GLOUCESTER RFC FROM
PILKINGTON
TO POWERGEN

GLOUCESTER RFC FROM PILKINGTON TO POWERGEN

IAN RANDALL

FOREWORD BY
NIGEL MELVILLE

Best Wishes,

Ian Randall

TEMPUS

To Mum and Dad

FRONTISPIECE: Partisan support: Gloucester fans
celebrating on the pitch at Kingsholm.

First published 2003

Tempus Publishing Ltd
The Mill, Brimscombe Port
Stroud, Gloucestershire GL5 2QG
www.tempus-publishing.com

© Ian Randall, 2003

British Library Cataloguing in Publication Data.
A catalogue record for this book is available from the British Library.

ISBN 0 7524 3120 X

Typesetting and origination by Tempus Publishing.
Printed in Great Britain by Midway Colour Print, Wiltshire.

CONTENTS

ACKNOWLEDGEMENTS

I would like to thank the following people who enabled this project to get from the ideas stage to a finished product, especially as I had never attempted anything like it before.

The thoughts of almost forty people are in the book. The long list of those who kindly gave their time for interviews included Jake Boer, Don Caskie, Chris Catling, Barrie Corless, Terry Fanolua, Bob Fenton, Rob Fidler, Tim Holder, Nigel Melville, John Neary, Ken Nottage, Dave Sims, Ian Smith, Graham Spring, Alistair Thomson, Peter Tocknell and Phil Vickery. Nigel's acceptance of my invitation to write the foreword was also much appreciated.

I was fortunate to have access to some invaluable BBC archive material. My thanks are due to Radio Gloucestershire station editor Mark Hurrell for that, and for allowing me the time away from my radio duties to write the text on a BBC computer. His active interest may have had something to do with him being a Gloucester RFC season-ticket holder! I must also acknowledge the contribution of Ian Mean, editor at the *Citizen*, who kindly allowed me the use of the paper's extensive back copy and photographic library. My thanks are also due to sports editor Mark Halliwell for some technical advice along the way, and to Bruce Seabrook at GPA Images for supplying the more modern photographs. I'm also grateful for the input of the official Zurich statistician, Stuart Farmer at SFMS Ltd, who supplied all the statistics.

The following publications were also used for reference:
   125 Glorious Years 1873-1998 compiled by Andrew Harley
   Kingsholm 1891-1991 by Peter Arnold
   Cup Final programme 1990 – Gloucester *v* Bath
   Cup Final programme 2003 – Gloucester *v* Northampton

I first met James Howarth and Kate Wiseman at Tempus Publishing in mid-May. Their backing of the concept and their help in delivering it has been much appreciated; especially considering the many phone calls a first-time author makes on what may seem the most minor point.

Lastly, I'm indebted to you, the reader, for buying the book. I hope you enjoy it.

Ian Randall,
October 2003

FOREWORD

When Ian offered me the opportunity to write a foreword for his forthcoming book on Gloucester, I jumped at the chance. Having been born and raised in Yorkshire, I am what my mother would have called a 'comer-in'. It could take up to twenty years for some people to be made welcome in our village!

My welcome in Gloucester was nothing more or less than I expected. The recent departure of Philippe Saint-André had fuelled emotions, and I only realise now that it was the size of the challenge and a fascination for this great, traditional rugby club that made me take the job. I had heard so many stories. A proud club with passionate support, a club that stood for more than just a game but a whole community: Gloucester Rugby Club was everything I believed a rugby club should stand for. How privileged I have been to play just a small part.

This book catalogues events at Gloucester during one of the most traumatic periods for the game of rugby union since the creation of what we know as modern rugby league back in 1906. The tale begins in the 'good old' amateur days where Glaws legends such as Mike Teague cleaned the mud off their boots after training with an old Bath shirt from the back of his van. As rugby union moved swiftly towards professionalism, Ian remembers those who worked so hard to ensure Gloucester stayed at the top of the national game. Keeping pace with everything required brave leaders and some tough decisions. There ensued the dawning of the new professional era, the arrival of Tom Walkinshaw and the acquisition of a host of international stars.

The story ends with the 2003 Powergen Cup final at Twickenham, which is a day that I will never forget. It was a day in the sun for everybody involved in the modern club game. There was a 75,000 capacity crowd at Twickenham for a match between two club sides. It was an occasion that had everything – colour, passion, excitement, quality and no little emotion. Walking around the pitch with the players, cup in hand, waving to a sea of cherry and white, was an emotional moment for everyone to savour.

This is not a story about the mere rugby club, but a tale of a community fighting its way through dark times to win its place in the sun. It's a story that will go on and on.

Nigel Melville
Director of Rugby, Gloucester RFC

PREFACE

September 1987. Margaret Thatcher was Prime Minister, Rick Astley was top of the charts and *Dirty Dancing* and *Fatal Attraction* were box-office hits at the cinema. Oh, and on the first Saturday of the new Courage League, Gloucester, captained by Marcus Hannaford, beat Coventry at Kingsholm by a score of 39-3. Until that season competitive rugby outside the international sphere had been confined to three areas. These were the County Championship, the traditional tier above the club game, and two club competitions – the John Player Cup, introduced in 1972, and merit tables, where clubs weren't forced to alter long-standing fixture lists. Such tables were judged on a winning percentage rather than the number of points. The concept of a genuine League though, containing eleven teams, shifted the emphasis and gave the game a greater focus.

Of the clubs that formed that inaugural division, four, including Gloucester, have been ever-present since. The other three are Bath, Harlequins and Wasps. Gloucester's record that season – six wins, one draw and three defeats – fully justified their inclusion in a system where each team only played each other once. The city had traditionally been the most prominent centre of population where football played second fiddle to rugby. Bath had been a small club until as little as ten years previously, whereas Gloucester had built up an earthy yet knowledgeable reputation, based in no small measure on the success of the Gloucestershire side in the County Championship – Gloucester and Bristol usually provided almost all the players. Lancashire and Yorkshire were other strong supporters of County rugby, but in both those areas football was king. Ranking alongside them was Cornwall, but the club game in the West Country had such an insular rivalry that one of them alone could never make an impact. The steady rise of Penzance & Newlyn, however, may soon change that.

Rugby in Gloucester is best viewed as a mini pyramid, with the Cherry & Whites at the top. More people play the game per head of population than anywhere else in the country, and on sheer volume alone, the likelihood was that players with natural talent would either be invited to Kingsholm or take their chance in a pre-season trial. In the same way that Yorkshire County Cricket Club would traditionally shout down a coal mine if they wanted a fast bowler, Gloucester had enough players within walking distance of their home ground not to be short of cover. Other clubs weren't so fortunate in having such a strong local infrastructure.

Support for the club has always been plentiful, although it is arguably more widespread now than ever before. Gloucester moved to Kingsholm from the Spa, the home of the city's cricket club, in 1891. The plot purchased was part of the Castle Grim Estate, and its proximity to the city centre and ease of access has no doubt helped to maintain the club's bond with the residents, a bond which may be lost if the club were ever to move to a concrete rectangle somewhere on the perimeter.

The Courage League was formed after a notable period in Gloucester's history. The club had a string of internationals in the 1970s, and they had twice won the John Player Cup, before sharing it in a drawn final with Moseley in 1982. A promising back row called Teague was beginning to make his mark, and it seemed only a matter of time before Gloucester would again be picking up some major silverware. As things turned out, the wait was rather longer than everybody thought.

THE FINAL AND
THE FALL OUT

CLASSIC MATCH 1

5 May 1990, Twickenham, Pilkington Cup (Final), Bath 48 Gloucester 6

Dazzling Bath tore Gloucester apart to lift the Pilkington Cup after Gloucester gifted them a string of needless scores in the first half and never recovered in sunny conditions which could not have been better for Bath's much vaunted back division. It was a day when too many Gloucester players were off form and failed to do themselves justice on the big occasion.

The ground began to echo with the chants of a huge Gloucester support a full 90 minutes before kick off, and the passion of vintage Gloucester was evident in the opening minutes as Mike Teague struck an important psychological blow by beating Dave Egerton to the ball in the first line-out. Tim Smith then cleanly took a towering up-and-under from Simon Halliday, but a moment's lapse in concentration saw Bath open the scoring. Flanker Kevin Withey took the ball at a line-out on the halfway line, and shrugged off several tackles as he charged towards the Gloucester line. Mike Hamlin failed to shove him into touch and Tim Smith couldn't reach him before he scored. Stuart Barnes converted and added a penalty shortly afterwards as Gloucester failed to release the ball in the tackle.

They were still trailing 9-0 when Malcolm Preedy appeared to stamp on Gareth Chilcott midway through the first half. Referee Fred Howard spoke to Preedy and skipper Hamlin, but only awarded a penalty which Barnes missed. Two other efforts had gone wide as well by the time Jeremy Guscott glided through the Gloucester three-quarter line, and took a return pass from Tony Swift to score. Barnes converted, and by half-time Bath were virtually out of sight with two more tries in the last seven minutes before the interval. First Tim Smith fumbled an up-and-under which was hacked on by Jon Callard, who won the race for the touchdown, and then, as Gloucester finally looked threatening, Tony Swift intercepted a pass by Smith intended for Jim Breeze. He ran the length of the pitch to score, with Barnes adding the extra points.

Gloucester's best spell came in the period immediately after half-time. Barnes had kicked an early penalty for Bath, but a series of drives set up by Marcus Hannaford and Ian Smith finally saw Kevin Dunn peel away and dive over. Tim Smith converted. Gloucester were at last on the scoreboard, but then suffered the misery of losing flanker John Gadd, who was sent off by referee Howard for stamping. They had to play the last 25 minutes with fourteen men, and after one sizzling run by Breeze, the Bath siege on the Gloucester line was re-established. Their three quarters were a constant threat and it was no surprise` when Swift linked with Callard to run in for his second try of the match, and then the floodgates opened. Flanker Withey created a gap to leave hooker Graham Dawe to score easily under the posts, lock Nigel Redman took Bath's try count to seven, and prop Victor Ubogu robbed Derrick Morgan for another just before the whistle. Barnes converted two of the three tries that came in the last eight minutes, leaving Gloucester on the end of the biggest final defeat in the nineteen-year history of the competition.

People still mumble about it now.

The words of Ian Smith, the former Gloucester flanker and Scotland international, as he muses on what happened on the final Saturday of Gloucester's 1989/90 season. Thirteen years on, the Cherry & Whites' defeat by Bath is still discussed – although the current side have done their best to dim it in the memory of those who were supporters then, and are still supporters now. The 1989/90 result was a double disappointment, coming as it did seven days after a defeat at Nottingham which cost Gloucester the Courage League title. A season that promised so much had seen them end up with nothing.

The domestic knockout cup had been introduced in 1972, at a time when Gloucester had a very strong side. Despite being drawn away in every round, they reached Twickenham along with Moseley. Gloucester emerged as victors by a score of 17-6, the midlands club having had their England lock Nigel Horton sent off early in the first half. The official attendance for the match was a modest 10,500, although as former Gloucester and England prop Mike Burton recalls, the competition nearly didn't happen at all.

The RFU were against it, because they thought it might cause the wrong types to come to Twickenham. When we got to the final, we were told that the winning captain would collect the trophy and leave immediately, so there are no photographs of Mike Nicholls lifting the cup. He was off down the stairs, and as I recall the RFU officials looked like the men from the Kremlin. It wasn't much different when we murdered Leicester 6-3 in 1978.

Gloucester were indeed one of the cup specialists until Bath's domination began in 1984. At the time only Leicester could better their record of two wins and a share of the honours after a drawn final, again against Moseley, in 1982. The 1990 final was to be Gloucester's first since then, but Bath's sixth in seven seasons, and they had won all the other five. These were the days when Courage League matches were either home or away only, and certain pundits felt that rugby's administrators were struggling to keep pace with the game's developments. Money was coming in around the fringes, particularly where internationals were concerned.

As in 1972, the draw didn't favour Gloucester from the outset. They entered the competition at the last 32 stage, and despite a difficult draw, away to Wasps, sneaked a 23-19 win. They didn't know it then, but they were to get to Twickenham without setting foot on Kingsholm in the cup.

Next stop was Gosforth, twice winners of the cup in the mid-seventies. Gloucester won 26-15 in the north east, and then toppled out Nottingham at Beeston 26-16 in the

Richard Mogg: scorer of the winning
try in the third round at Wasps.

quarter-finals, a result they were to tellingly avenge in Gloucester's final league fixture. The semi-final, at Northampton, was won 17-12. Bath, meanwhile, had seen off Harlequins and Headingley at home before convincing wins at Richmond and Moseley took them to Twickenham. Once both sides had made the final, however, the build-up was very different, as Ian Smith, who was to make his 200th Gloucester appearance in the final, remembers only too well.

Bath couldn't win the league and so they had rested some of their side for the last few games. They had travelled up the night before the final, and so didn't have that journey on the day, like we did. It was a hot day, and there we were, sat on the M4 in a traffic jam in our crimplene blazers, bought for us all by Eric Vick (a staunch supporter). It was classic Gloucester organisation, but we didn't know any different. We'd put in a lot of effort to get to the final, and we wanted to finish it off, but we'd lost at Nottingham in the league the previous Saturday, and missed out on the championship. I remember nobody moving for about three quarters of an hour in the dressing room after that game, nobody changed, nobody said anything. I'd never known it be like that before, and we didn't want to go through that again.

Smith, despite his experience, wasn't captain that day. That honour was Mike Hamlin's, the outside half being the last man from outside the pack to skipper the Cherry & Whites through a whole season.

We knew that if we gave players like Guscott, Barnes and Halliday room, they would revel in it. The thing was that we'd picked up a few injuries, and as the grounds got harder and the weather got better we started to suffer. Bath had a tremendous side, but we had beaten them earlier in the season in the league, and so were looking forward to playing them. We were a workmanlike side without many stars, but we had team commitment and feeling for each other and we wanted to get that right on the day.

Hamlin and team coach Keith Richardson were the most visible characters at the club to those outside the hard-core supporters. Richardson was a former captain himself, and played as a prop when the author was first taken to Kingsholm by his father. He taught at Wycliffe College, possessed a dry wit, and wasn't prone to over-the-top outbursts. His observations in a BBC interview on the eve of the final were typical.

I would like us to enjoy playing at Twickenham in front of 50,000 people. If you don't it's sad. I would like to win, and at five o'clock, have the players just about managing to breathe properly, so that they've given everything, and done well enough to say that, for the right reasons, that's 80 minutes of my life I'll never forget.

Ultimately, nothing was to be further from the truth for a side drawn, in the majority, from Gloucester itself. Kevin Dunn's solitary try, converted by Tim Smith, was a paltry reward, but on the day, Gloucester didn't help themselves. Flanker John Gadd was sent off, there was that morning journey, even their footwear for the day wasn't the right choice. Don Caskie played at centre in the final at the end of his first season at the club.

I remember my feet being raw at the end of the match. We had been given new boots for the final and stupidly wore them. Most of us hadn't been to a final before, so we wore what we were given, and the skin was literally peeling off my feet. That Gloucester side was the most formidable one I ever played in, but on the day Bath were good and we were chasing shadows. It was one of Keith Richardson's sayings that nothing would happen in twenty minutes. We'd started OK and then Kevin Withey broke from the back of a line-out and scored. Bath never looked back after that.

While Caskie had wave upon wave of Bath attacks to deal with, it was no easier in the forwards. Despite a powerful combination throughout, lock John Brain acknowledged that it was a game too far at the end of a long season.

Playmaker: Bath fly-half
Stuart Barnes.

Feeling the heat: Tim Smith watches a high ball with Marcus Hannaford and Bath's Tony Swift.

I remember it was a hot day, and as Richard Hill told me when he came to Kingsholm as director of rugby, Bath would always try a bit harder against Gloucester. They took considerable delight in beating us. I think they had eleven internationals and we had two – Malcolm Preedy and Mike Teague – and on the day everything clicked for them. We were a good unit but we were out on our feet. I can remember walking out and being hit by this wall of sound. It made the hairs stand up on the back of your neck. It was a great day – apart from the result.

Gloucester's defeat left them with nothing to show for their season's work. Just a fortnight after being hailed as the best team the club had ever had, some tagged them the worst. If they had managed to secure either of the two honours that were so nearly theirs, would the course of history be any different? We'll never know, but as Ian Smith thinks back, there was no major self analysis.

It would have been good for the players and management to sit down and ask what did go wrong. Had it been done a month after the final, it might have moved the club forward sooner, but Gloucester was a very traditional club. Quite a few players were getting towards the end of their careers. They had given a lot and it was hard to leave them out of the team, and even harder for someone to have the balls to stand up and say something. There were a lot of old players on the committee and very few new faces joined in that group.

So it was for the next two seasons. Keith Richardson remained as coach, but there was a change of captain, with Smith replacing Mike Hamlin in the summer of 1991. At that stage John Gadd returned to Stroud and Dave Spencer went to Lydney, but the core of the side remained. World Cup year brought memorable matches against England and an Irish Presidents XV to celebrate one hundred years of rugby at Kingsholm, but League form remained mixed. The following year, Gloucester finished in fourth place, and there

was another chance to reach Twickenham when Bath provided the opposition in a semi-final. This, though, was to be a punctuation point in the club's history. Despite a solid season, twelve players left Gloucester that summer. Not surprisingly, the list included some distinguished names. Mike Hamlin and Nigel Scrivens went to London Welsh, Mike Teague joined Moseley, Kevin Dunn, who still lived in Gloucester, linked up with Wasps and Malcolm Preedy and Richard Mogg moved to Cheltenham. For Teague, it was to be a third sojourn away from Kingsholm after spells at Stroud and Cardiff.

I couldn't leave the club on a higher note than leading my country out against them on my home ground. I wanted to leave Kingsholm at the top, and to be remembered as, dare I say, a favourite. I had been injured for quite a while and the club had done quite nicely without me.

It wasn't a view shared by Mickey Booth. Booth had played over 400 games for Gloucester as a scrum half, and he had just taken over from Alan Brinn as chairman of selectors.

My immediate worry was that our strength in depth had disappeared. It would have been nice for Mike Hamlin to look after our United backs. Richard Mogg, who I regarded very highly, could have worked with our outside backs, and Nigel Scrivens could have done a great job bringing through Richard West. We lost a few but as always the spirit in the club remained, and I remember thinking that it would be nice to do well in the league and the cup with a home-grown team.

A lot of responsibility was being placed on the experienced players that remained. One of them was centre Don Caskie.

If you looked under the veneer of it all, a lot of that group had come to the end of their time, and no-one ever wants to admit that. We had tried to replace the quality players that got us to the 1990 final, but there was nothing coming through, and there wasn't a real fear of being dropped. I can remember having a long run in the first team from that point onwards. I stayed at the club until 1997, and I probably only played about a dozen games for the United side.

The alarm bells were soon ringing. Three of the first four league games ended in defeat before the visit of bottom side West Hartlepool to Kingsholm. A 21-6 reversal didn't do much for the health of coach Keith Richardson, and his post-match thoughts were as pithy as usual.

I didn't see anything in that performance that holds any hope whatsoever. All I hope is that it serves as something to galvanise the players into producing something better. We can't play like that again. If that's all we are capable of producing we'll never beat anyone in Division One again. That has to serve as the lowest point, and to embarrass everyone associated with the club to the point where we say we've got to do better than that.

Initially, it didn't happen. Cup interest was ended at Newcastle Gosforth before Christmas, but a spirited second half of the season brought away wins at London Irish, Northampton and Bristol. The campaign ended with a huge sigh of relief after a 25-5 victory over Harlequins at Kingsholm and the long-serving Richardson put the season into perspective.

Gloucester is a club that weathers storms, and not many would have had our injury list and come through. In truth we got away with it. The British have got a tradition for getting thumped in a battle and commemorating it as a success, and in many ways it was a success. Normally at the end of the season you think 'thank goodness for that' but that season felt like it was fifty years, and I'm sure it wasn't only me. It was nearly a disaster. It could be one of Gloucester's most important seasons, a watershed if you like. We mustn't bury our heads in the sand. We must formulate a plan and say this is where our development is going. We must look at what might happen in three, four

OPPOSITE ABOVE: Struggling: Mike Hamlin tries to cover another Bath attack set-up by Jeremy Guscott.

RIGHT:
Iron Mike: Mike Teague hard at work in the gym.

or five years. We've had a meeting with the players and we've let them know what is going on. The club is going to appoint a rugby supremo.

From the outside this looked like a giant leap. While other teams had been recruiting on a national level for a couple of years, Gloucester had relied on talent coming through in pre-season trials and from local clubs. Now, they were preparing to potentially open their doors to an external candidate for this new role. The chairman at the time was Peter Ford.

We had actually toyed with the idea for some while. Even three or four years before, I felt we should have looked at it. It was getting ever more time-consuming to run the club, and we were looking for someone to take charge of the whole system, which is why there was the job title director of rugby. The playing side and the administration of the playing side was the main thing, but we wanted someone to come in and put us where we felt we should be. We had looked at things from an amateur point of view but the picture was changing rapidly. It was the only way we could go.

Also in on those early conversations had been team coach Keith Richardson and Ian Smith, who had just been voted in as captain for a third season by his fellow players, and who by now was a Scottish international.

Keith and I had sat down at the end of the 1991/92 season and discussed where the club was going. I had a lot of time for Keith, and we still chat now, more than ten years later. We felt we needed to take a leaf out of other people's books and get someone in to organise the rugby properly. I was encouraged. Some of the other players looked a bit shocked and surprised, but it was a fresh beginning. The players knew there would be less club rugby the following season because the league was moving to both home and away games. They also knew they needed to be more professional in their attitude, and that was a shock to one or two, but there was going to be someone employed full time to get the best out of them.

Laying down the law: Keith Richardson (left) with a young Dave Sims.

Senior men: Gloucester club chairman Peter Ford (LEFT) and skipper Ian Smith (RIGHT).

Gloucester had realised that to become a major force in the top division, change was critical. There was no feeling of crisis, but there was a desire to act quickly and accept new ideas, ideas that would cost money – money that would be found. There had been a perception in the past that the grass was greener at other clubs, but Keith Richardson had drummed into the players that it was a myth after a dinner during the season where he had sat down and compared notes. Gloucester *did* do as much, if not more than other teams, and that support would get better. Perhaps Gloucester hadn't sold themselves as a club as well as they might have done, and if ever there was any doubt about the need for an extra pair of hands to steer the ship, Keith Richardson spelled it out – knowing he might be a loser in the whole equation.

Coaching a team as an enthusiastic amateur is one thing, but there are other jobs to be fitted in around it. Tony Russ at Leicester used to spend the whole of his Monday editing the match video from the previous Saturday. That won't wait. There are training programmes to be sorted out with a fitness advisor. You need to be aware of who the best young players are by watching games, and then perhaps talking to those players. I enjoy coaching, but I don't have the time to devote most of my social life to Gloucester Rugby Club. I just try to do the job to the best of my ability, and if we do well and someone says 'well done' over a pint you accept it. I also know that things can be the opposite way round as well. I could have talked myself out of a nice coaching job. Whoever they appoint might not want Keith Richardson as a coach.

Richardson needn't have worried. His experience as a head coach, which extended back to the start of the Courage Leagues and up a level with his attachment to the England A squad was retained by Gloucester's first director of rugby. He started work on 1 July 1993. His name? Barrie Corless.

THE
CORLESS
ERA

CLASSIC MATCH 2

17 December 1994, College Grove, Wakefield, Pilkington Cup (Round 4)
Wakefield 19 Gloucester 9

Gloucester crashed out of the Pilkington Cup with a disappointing defeat after a poor performance at Courage Division Two side Wakefield. Gloucester had the talent to beat their Yorkshire opponents, but despite winning enough line-out ball to dominate any match, they failed to use it effectively and rarely created any scoring chances. It was a day when their tactics let them down. They didn't take the game to Wakefield as they had promised to do, their kicking out of hand was poor and partly because of that, they chose to run penalties when kicking for the corners would have been the better option.

The only scores in the first half were three penalties. Full-back Mark Mapletoft, who saw one attempt strike an upright and bounce away, kicked an early goal after Wakefield were offside, and added a second on the half hour. By that stage the Wakefield captain Mike Jackson had brought his side level at 3-3 with one successful kick, but Gloucester had also had a try disallowed. An excellent catch by Richard West set up a chance for Paul Holford to break through the midfield. Holford fed Simon Morris, who then set up the opportunity for wing Lee Osborne to touch down, only for referee Cousins to rule there had been a forward pass. It was to be Gloucester's clearest opportunity, and they finished the half on the defensive as Paul Holford made an important tackle on wing Richard Thompson as he closed in on the Gloucester line.

Wakefield had the encouragement of playing down the slope in the second half, and within ten minutes Jackson, who had missed three penalties in the first half, took his fifth chance of the match to make it 6-6. Gloucester seemed unable to get any sort of penetrative move going, and were having to play the game largely in their own half. There was a sense of panic creeping in as Wakefield prevented them from crossing the gain line, and the Cherry & Whites started to run the ball from almost all corners of the ground. Their defences were finally breached when a powerful run by centre Andy Metcalfe (who later played for Gloucester) saw him burst through the Gloucester cover and put skipper Jackson in for an unconverted try.

Gloucester still had twenty minutes to save the situation, and fly-half Martyn Kimber dropped a goal to reduce the deficit, but two long-range penalty chances for Mapletoft came and went without success. They were still two points down when for once they lost their own ball in the line-out, and Wakefield moved the ball wide for Thompson to score in the corner. Gloucester now needed a converted try to tie the scores, but a last-minute drop goal by Wakefield fly-half Richard Petyt buried any hopes Gloucester had of scrambling a last gasp victory.

(On the same day, Gloucester's near neighbours Lydney were drawn to play at Sandal, about four miles from Wakefield. Lydney won 17-5, before also losing to Wakefield in the fifth round at Regentsholm.)

Barrie Corless was forty-seven years old when he came to Gloucester. He had won ten England caps as a centre between 1976 and 1978, and played all his rugby for three midland clubs: Birmingham, Coventry and Moseley. When he finished playing, he was employed by the RFU as a regional coach, but it was what he had achieved at Northampton that made others sit up and take notice. He went there in 1988 after the Saints committee was voted out at the AGM. The new one brought Corless in, and in five seasons as a director of coaching he took them from the lower reaches of Division Two to a solid position in Division One, and their first domestic Cup final, where they eventually lost to Harlequins after extra time. His initial contract at Northampton was up in the summer of 1993, and although the club was still developing, it was the nagging doubt that topping the progress he had made would be difficult, along with some background networking by Gloucester chairman Peter Ford, that planted the idea of a move to Gloucester in Corless' mind.

It was Chalky White at Leicester who first had a word with me on Peter's behalf. I laughed it off at the time but when he mentioned it a second time I was intrigued. I had played at Gloucester a few times and knew about its history and tradition. I knew they were having a poor time in terms of results but there was that 'what if we could get it right' challenge about it. I never actually knew if anyone else was in for the job or not. I met Peter Ford, and then met him again with Alan Brinn, and the deal was done. Peter very much ran the club at that time. I remember Jim Jarrett telling me he'd been vice-chairman for ten years and he'd never made a decision! I never had a contract or a job description. It was very informal.

One of the best stories, and it still does the rounds now, concerns the England international Mike Catt. Catt could have been a Gloucester player, but when he first rang the club no-one answered the phone. The chance was gone and he ended up at Bath. Recruitment and structuring the playing side of the club was an important idea in the mind of Peter Ford, and Corless had a good reputation having brought through several high quality players at Franklins Gardens. He had spotted Nick Beal playing for junior club High Wycombe: Tim Rodber, Paul Grayson and Matt Dawson all signed during his time there, and he developed the career of another powerful runner for England, Ian Hunter. Northampton couldn't survive on local talent, so had to look elsewhere, and although that had been Gloucester's strength, the mentality seemed to be shifting. The view of Gordon Sargent, a former prop with one England cap, was typical.

Gloucester is a rugby-mad city but we weren't going to produce all the quality players you need season in, season out from Gloucester itself. There were probably enough to make the core of a good

RIGHT:

Historic day: Barrie Corless
starts work, 1 July 1993.

BELOW:

Fighting talk: Barrie Corless
shares a joke with coach Keith
Richardson.

*side IF you could get them young enough and point them in the right direction. We needed a net
to make sure we didn't miss anyone locally and then if you couldn't find a certain type of player
you would look further afield. The Colts and the Under-21s are where you start from and the better
the foundations, the higher you go.*

It was a model Barrie Corless had honed at Northampton with the backing of the new
committee, but he was to find Gloucester still with an 'old school' approach. John Fidler
and Eric Stephens were two men at Gloucester young enough to have played against
Corless, but the majority of the committee were from a previous era. They disliked
change, and wanted things done in the way they had been in the past, and even getting
little things through proved difficult. Reg Collins, the former club president, ran the
Colts in those days. They trained on a Monday, and usually played on a Wednesday.
Barrie wanted to get the side to play on a Saturday, and had to present a paper to the
committee to try and convince them. It was the only committee meeting he ever
attended.

*My argument was the lads were only getting team organisation to play matches, and we had no time
to coach them and make them better players. I didn't think it was in the best interests of the club.
I always felt if all the individuals in a team improved by 10 per cent then the effect on the team
would be huge. As a coach I always tried to develop individual skills, and then put them into
opposed situations and combine decision making as well. I was told there were reasons why we
couldn't have colt games on a Saturday, and in my mind the main reason was that Reg Collins
liked to watch the first XV. That to me was the wrong reason.*

Corless retained the services of Keith Richardson, who had coached the first team since the leagues began, and after a pre-season tour to Italy, Gloucester started the 1993/94 season with two draws, one at home to Wasps, and another away at Newcastle Gosforth. Richardson's time at the club meant he had a vast amount of knowledge and respect, and while Barrie was trying to harness that in his own way, it became clear breaking into that group wasn't going to be easy for an outsider. The one man who did know him was the centre Don Caskie.

Barrie had approached me to go to Northampton from Gloucester. It was in the days when there was a job offer tied in as well, but I stayed put. I had a lot of respect for Keith Richardson. He knew how the club worked, how it ticked, and how to get everybody onside. He was a good talker, knew all the players really well, and wouldn't ask you to do anything he didn't think you were capable of. Barrie had his own ideas and was good at technical drills but didn't seem to get into the heart of the club or what it was about. Some coaches you hit it off with, and some you don't, and he didn't do it for me.

Ian Smith, now approaching 300 matches for Gloucester, was captain in Corless' first season.

Keith had the right psychology for us. He hit us at the right level, and was always taking the **** out of us and himself. Barrie didn't seem to say the right things. I don't remember him as a motivator at all.

Those early months were tough in terms of results. Gloucester had to wait until 20 November for their first league win, the 19-14 victory (ironically over Northampton) following four straight defeats. The hardest one for Corless to stomach was the one at Bath, where former England international Stuart Barnes saw an unrecognisable Gloucester side.

You don't associate Gloucester with a lack of passion, and there was a lack of passion in that performance. It's a tough league now, and Gloucester must get the fire and hunger back or else they will be in difficulties.

Corless' view was no different.

One of the things I didn't foresee when I came to Gloucester was a lack of commitment from fifteen players on the field. A lot of that comes from a lack of confidence, and that comes from a lack of leadership, and I don't mean from Ian Smith. Not enough of our good players are playing well, and it's feeding onto the rest of the team.

One of his protégés at Northampton, Ian Hunter, didn't see Corless fixing all Gloucester's problems at a stroke.

Barrie went to Kingsholm with a big reputation but people forget how long it took him to get us into Division One and then established there. He was very dedicated and had the eye for a good player. Everyone expects results straight away but success doesn't happen overnight.

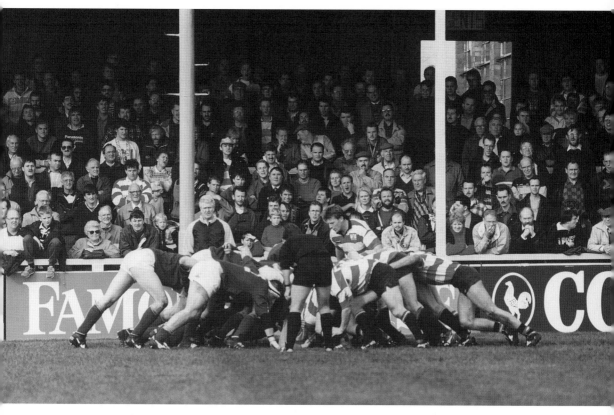

Gloucester v. London Irish, October 1993. By modern standards, a sparsely populated Shed looks on.
Gloucester lost the match 10-9.

By now the league profile was increasing several times over and with home and away matches in place for the first time, recruitment was becoming more competitive. The well oiled machine that Corless built at Northampton had brought in the likes of John Etheridge (from Gloucester) and England hooker John Olver, who was found a teaching post at a local grammar school. Now he was dealing with a very different animal.

When I played at Gloucester I always felt they were a bit remote as a club. Players and committee kept themselves to themselves, and it was never the most welcoming. I felt we had to modernise the whole club, and that was a big challenge. We had to be more proactive and sell the club in a better way in order to get new players. Northampton had a committee man who pulled some well-connected businessmen together to make sure jobs were found for players, and David Foyle (who later became Chairman of the Board of Directors) did that for me at Gloucester, but it takes a year or two to get those systems working for you.

As it was, just three new players made their league debuts for Gloucester in Corless' first season – Bruce Fenley, Ashley Johnson, who might have played more had he not suffered a broken leg, and Ben Maslen. The best run of form came either side of

25

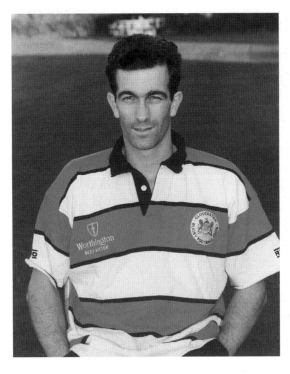

Martyn Kimber: dropped 12 goals in thirty-nine league appearances, but his cup effort at Wakefield couldn't prevent a shock defeat.

Christmas, with four wins out of five in the league, along with Pilkington Cup victories away at Nottingham and at home against Northampton, where Corless' inside knowledge again proved useful. Leicester broke the run at Welford Road, and Gloucester won only two of their last six league games, as well as losing 10-3 to Orrell at Kingsholm in a cup quarter-final. They finished the season in eighth place, and said goodbye to Keith Richardson, who after twenty-six years as a player and latterly a coach, left to join Harlequins.

Going to Quins showed my perverse sense of humour really. They were a team we'd all knocked over the years, but they were a club with a lot of star players. They were a glamorous club, if you like, and that image appealed to me.

Richardson's departure left Corless to bring in another forwards coach, and it fell to another former player, Viv Wooley, to fill the role having cut his coaching teeth at Gloucester Old Boys. The most notable acquisition on the playing side was Mark Mapletoft, a small but chunky full back who kicked his goals and had the eye for a gap in open play. Corless had first seen him as a sixteen-year-old and had kept tabs on him after he'd gone to university at Loughborough. Locks Mark Cornwell and Rob Fidler were breaking through, and Martyn Kimber, Lee Osborne and Adey Powels maintained the tradition of good local players finding their way to Kingsholm, but still there was no star name and problems with confidence amongst the squad remained. It was a situation Corless found hard to fathom.

Lee Osborne, kicker of 3 penalties in the win over Leicester.

We had a core of established players who could do a job at that level but for such a robust team, there wasn't much self belief. I don't know if that is a reflection of the city or not. Having got the game by the scruff of the neck, they didn't seem to be able to turn the screw. It was almost as if they didn't know how to win. Losing had become a bit of a habit and although we had the likes of Paul Holford and Simon Morris there was nobody who was a real match winner, who could turn a close game, or a dominant character, like I had with Wayne Shelford at Northampton. He had finished his international career, and was looking to coach as well as play, and he was a great figure in terms of developing those around him. Tim Rodber became a good player much faster for both Northampton and England because of Shelford.

The pre-season tour ahead of the 1994/95 season saw Gloucester go to South Africa, and then return home to be trounced 45-8 by Wasps at Sudbury. Six tries followed the week after at home to West Hartlepool, only for the optimism to evaporate again at Leicester. The telling tale of that season was how many of the league results were close – Gloucester's last nine Courage League fixtures under Corless were all decided by six points or less. It was a wider margin than that at Wakefield in the cup, but the wrong way as Gloucester were dumped out of the competition by lower league opposition. On his own admission, it was the worst performance of the team while he was in charge.

The experienced players played with a total lack of thought and tactical nous. We were like a school side. They were more keyed up than we were and it was almost as if we went up there expecting to win, and unless we gave 100 per cent we weren't good enough to win. We had to change the style of play because although the pack was adequate, once other teams were on a par with us we needed something else. We were trying to develop a wider game and because we were a bit plain at 10 and in the centre, we tried to get the wingers into the midfield a lot more, but that day we were dreadful. I'd actually arranged a lift home but felt I shouldn't desert the ship after the way we'd played and so decided to go back to Gloucester on the coach with the players. What I forgot to do was tell them, so the coach left without me and I had to make my way home on the train.

Barrie Corless had clearly expected an improvement in his second season at Gloucester, but that improvement never materialised on a consistent basis. Bath and Leicester were still setting the benchmarks, while Corless was still striving to break down mental barriers at Kingsholm. The approach amongst the players seemed to be that a victory took the pressure off the next week, rather than trying to build on one win and make it two, three or four in a row. Off the field too, he sensed that not everyone was pulling in the same direction.

I was Gloucester's first full-time organiser of the rugby at the club. The committee ran the club but I felt the vision of the way forward was never any more than Peter Ford's, and I was never sure how many of the committee bought into it, which was totally different from how it was at Northampton. Everybody there was on the same wavelength. Apart from the issue over the Colts, the kit deal was another little niggle. To me the pressures on the first team were greater, so first-team players should get a full set of kit, and United players a smaller selection, then after so many first-team appearances you got a first-team set of kit. Previously everybody had been treated the same. Ian Smith, as captain, was behind it but a few lads didn't like it, and when players moan to the committee it's very easy for the boat to start rocking.

Barrie Corless' last match at Gloucester was on 11 February 1995, when Gloucester beat Leicester 9-3 at Kingsholm. Gloucester played thirty league matches under his tutelage, winning eleven, drawing two, and losing seventeen. His plan, twenty months down the line, clearly wasn't the finished article, but it would be hard to argue against a committee who said performances on the field weren't good enough given those statistics. He was quickly employed by his old club Moseley after leaving Kingsholm, and now splits his time between various rugby projects. He coaches at the Sixth Form College in Solihull and at King Edward's School in Stratford, as well as helping at Moseley and developing his own coaching website. He also made profitable use of the severance package from Kingsholm, which he used to buy a house for students at Birmingham University. It doubled in value in four years, and Corless sold it and bought four houses in Burnley that he still owns with the proceeds.

He still loves rugby, but concedes that at 57, the only job that would take him back into the game on a full-time basis would be a role with an academy, where he could work with young players. That perhaps shows where Barrie Corless' strengths always lay – working on the training ground, sharpening skills, and if you had to assess his contribution at the club, it would be in his signing of Mark Mapletoft, who is still Gloucester's top scorer in league rugby (836 points from 75 appearances), and in shaking the club up for what was to follow – which, as it turned out, was pretty significant.

A YEAR OF CHANGE

The big bang in rugby union can be traced to two possible dates. Depending on your viewpoint, it was either 27 August 1995 or 4 May 1996. The first was the day Vernon Pugh, who led the International Rugby Board's investigation into professionalism, announced the game would become open. The second was the date where the top English clubs, including Gloucester, could start the scramble to sign players on professional contracts. Both, on different levels, were equally groundbreaking. Gloucester wanted to be ready for both.

Barrie Corless' departure left Viv Wooley to steer the players through the remainder of the 1994/95 season on the field, but Viv wasn't full time. Safety was achieved but off the field there was a change of gear. Speculation was rife about what might happen after the 1995 World Cup, and the club didn't want to be left behind. Peter Ford, who was chairman when Gloucester decided they needed their first full-time director of rugby, had now been replaced full time by Alan Brinn. The drive now was not to get a coach who could deal with administration, but an administrator who could support the playing side of the club. It was a shift in emphasis that saw Brinn and the committee looking towards London in the aftermath of Corless leaving Kingsholm.

The thinking within the club was this was only one part of the equation. We were revamping the coaching and selection over the summer, and hadn't rejected the idea of a rugby manager to oversee the team, but we needed a high-powered type of person to be our chief executive, and also replace Mike Burton on the commercial side. Through a chain of events, we approached Mike Coley, who had a background and contacts in rugby. The brief was to have someone looking after the big projects like the possible rebuilding of the main stand (still not done eight years later!) and solving our off-the-field problems, such as making sure young players we might target actually arrive.

Coley's background was indeed impressive. He had worked at the RFU for six years, and had commercially helped to pull in the funds to build the North Stand at Twickenham. It was that knowledge he wanted to put into Kingsholm, as well as steering the club through some choppy waters ahead.

Barrie Corless didn't do too badly, but it was time to look to the future. The regulations over players hit Gloucester harder than most teams. You couldn't just borrow a player from a combination club if you needed one because of the 120-day registration period before he could play. It meant you realistically had to sit down in the summer of 1995 and look at the strengths and weaknesses in the team you wanted to address for the start of the following season, twelve months on. Everything

Gloucester club chairman Alan Brinn (ABOVE) and new chief executive Mike Coley (RIGHT).

on the commercial side had to be geared towards the playing side because no senior club could sustain paying players a living wage at the time, and that was what we were going to be faced with. You could think about paying incentives, but that was all. The National Lottery was up and running and there was the chance of money for capital projects from that. I was really a filter – to help the rugby side of the club and give them the best possible facilities in all areas.

Mike Coley was just getting his feet under the table when Gloucester's two World Cup selections, Richard West and Ian Smith, were flying out with England and Scotland respectively, and another former England international was calling time on his playing career. Mike Teague, who had played in the 1991 World Cup final for England against Australia, played his 292nd and final match for the Cherry & Whites against Harlequins on the final day of the 1994/95 season. Teague had been educated at Churchdown School, where as an athlete he was selected to run for Cheltenham & District in the 400 metres. By the age of thirteen, he was playing rugby for the school, and his last games report spoke of a boy who had listened, worked hard on developing his skills, and could make a first-class no. 8! At the All Blues club in the city, where Teague played with his brother Gary, the walls of the skittle alley were adorned with memorabilia, and their appreciation of him was mirrored at the highest level after he starred in both the England and British Lions jersey between 1989 and 1992.

Will Carling (England captain): *Mike was one the most respected members of the team. He was a very private man, never seeking adulation but he was phenomenally strong and incredibly fit.*

Pack Ackford (England team mate): *Mike was wonderful to play alongside because he would get over the gain line, move guys aside and provide a target for you to hit. Along with Peter*

Winterbottom he was the hardest mental player I ever came across. You can judge that by looking into people's eyes – and Mike's were always sparking.

Roger Uttley (England coach): *Mike was a hardened and experienced campaigner, very professional in his approach, and someone who gave security and confidence to the team.*

Teague hung up his boots with a bank full of memories.

If people could imagine the fun I've got out of rugby, then they'd realise what a great game it is. I made so many friends, and during the 1991 World Cup we were getting good luck cards from all over the country. I remember one from a Gloucester City fan asking if I would be their new centre forward. I was one of the lucky ones to play in the final and meet the Queen. We came so close but the Australian defence was just too good and we couldn't break through. We felt we couldn't have done any more. At Gloucester, I enjoyed every minute. Personally I always thought I played my best rugby in a Cherry & White shirt. Whenever I picked up the ball there was this huge wealth of goodwill wanting me to succeed, and I took that with me all over the world. I was still enjoying it but the cracks were beginning to appear and it wouldn't have been long before the Shed let me know that. The one-off big challenges were OK but the league games were getting like mini internationals, and I was 35. We couldn't afford to be carrying individuals and it was time to move over.

Whichever way the game was to go, Gloucester felt they couldn't afford to let Teague just walk away, and by the time of the summer AGM, Alan Brinn had persuaded him, and another long-serving player, John Fidler, to become team manager and team secretary. This was an old guard solution with a professional game very much on the horizon, but one Brinn felt would call on some invaluable experience.

I chatted with Mike after the end of the season and although he said he didn't want to play, he indicated he would like to be involved. Initially it might just have been on the selection panel, but we gave him a title. We thought that would attract some attention and thought it would make people listen if they were told Mike Teague was on the phone. The idea was that he would work closely with the coach (Viv Wooley) and the captain (Dave Sims) and be responsible for selection, because one man couldn't do everything, and it meant we had three former internationals involved – Mike, John and Peter Kingston.

Fidler was to lend his support as a troubleshooter at the club right through until March 2000, and no one was more optimistic about the new set-up.

None of us were empire builders, and people realised what Mike had done. I thought he was the ideal person to be team manager. We played together and were close friends, but knew that the players needed to be committed and more professional, and that certain positions needed strengthening. We'd had a difficult season but people needed to stop criticising and start encouraging. No-one was more fed up than me about us bouncing along near the bottom of the table. I felt we ought to be in the top three.

Typical Teague: England and British Lions no. 8 Mike Teague as Gloucester fans will remember him.

A new playing and business structure was now in place, but the turbulent events earlier in the year had seen members come out in force at the AGM to express their views. The majority of a membership that was much smaller than the current level of season ticket sales seemed to accept headway was being made slowly, and there was even the prospect of an overseas centre – New Zealander, Frank Bunce – being lured to Kingsholm. By now West and Smith were back from the World Cup, having each played one match, but my diary notes for 25 July 1995 showed that the revamped Gloucester management could have a lot to cope with.

Fids for President? John Fidler (nearest camera) alongside Gareth Rees and John Brain.

In my inimitable scribble, I had noted that the RFU had announced a £30,000 package for each of England's top players because the Union were worried about a professional tour being put together by Kerry Packer, the Australian previously responsible for World Series Cricket. Contracts had been put to between 90 and 120 players, with regard to them playing in a circus separate from the Five Nations on a professional basis, although no Gloucester players were involved. Moreover, Rupert Murdoch had set up a multi-million pound deal involving South Africa, New Zealand and Australia playing in a Tri-Nations tournament that would start in 1996. The gauntlet had been thrown down, and former Gloucester and England prop Mike Burton felt the IRB meeting at the end of August would drive a hole through the word amateur at the top level.

What happened alerted the RFU and the International Rugby Board. The Packer scenario basically told England that they would have to offer the players some sort of professional contract to keep them. The set up was that 10 per cent of the Packer money would have been paid in the November, and the rest the following March, but I felt most of the England players would stay if they could keep their jobs and earn reasonable money playing professional rugby.

We didn't have to wait long for the International Rugby Board's findings concerning what should be done about amateurism. Vernon Pugh, who died earlier this year, was the man charged with leading the IRB investigation, and on 27 August 1995, a new age of professional rugby was trumpeted in with Pugh's historic statement.

Subsequent to the repeal of the amateur regulations, rugby will become an open game. There will be no prohibition on payment, or the provision of material benefit to any person involved in the game. It has also been agreed that payment may be made at any level of participation – that there should be no pay ceiling – and payment by results is not prohibited. The regulations will be permissive, not mandatory, and any Union in the membership may put in place domestic restrictions which may be more restrictive.

Sat in his office in Gloucester, Mike Coley saw the decision as a real can of worms.

The IRB took out all the stops from the amateur game, and we wanted guidance. Gloucester was always an amateur club and that was still the view of the committee. We were thrust into a state of flux, although we suspected things would blow up after the World Cup. At that stage we had already had four or five meetings to discuss the concept of a Premier League. We needed between £800,000 and £1 million a year to run each club or we wouldn't have a professional game, and I was concerned that you could have England players earning money through sponsorship deals while other players at the club were getting nothing. It looked very divisive.

The IRB decision had been taken after discussions between the twenty delegates in Paris, yet it appeared to have taken some by surprise. The mood among the journalists present was akin to that of a funeral, seeing the end of the game as they knew it, but

Still in the game: Mike Burton is now a successful agent, having played for Gloucester thirty years ago. (www.gpaimages.com)

In the mix: RFU secretary Tony Hallett.
(photograph courtesy of RFU).

John Jeavons Fellows, who represented the RFU, said the Union *would* assist clubs in their professional education.

One or two treasurers will be asking what they should do with the brown envelopes, but that's where we have to think of the implications from top to bottom. I see market forces taking hold. Those at the top who can afford to pay will, and the rest won't. It will concentrate a few minds but we see the majority of clubs, those who rely on membership fees, match fees and bar takings, staying amateur.

RFU secretary Tony Hallett was one of the men Mike Coley dealt with in his discussions regarding a Premier League, and even then, he could see the game needing the structure it has now.

The good men of Gloucestershire will want the best of the amateur ethos retained, even in an open game. Clubs will need support over matters such as transfer fees, but the 120-day registration period is in place, and that will help to give us a transition period, because otherwise we would see a strain on clubs' finances that they hadn't budgeted for. I also think we need another level of competition, something between club level and international level, possibly with European involvement. Funds would then come out of it in terms of sponsorship and television, and that could be directed to both those in it and below it, so that they don't fall behind. After 140 years we have now got to get used to paying for playing, but I think the most typical problem initially will be survival in your own league.

Clearly all this happening so close to the start of the season made it the talk of the Shed at the opening League game against Sale. Gloucester lost 22-17, and at Bath the following week, before the first win of the season away at West Hartlepool. All the while, Mike Coley and representatives from the other top teams were arguing they were a special group in the light of the IRB decision. They formed EFDR (English First Division Rugby) – an organisation involving well-respected names such as Peter Wheeler and Tony Russ – and as the season developed, the group had exhaustive discussions with the RFU. By January 1996, Coley was tearing his hair out.

EFDR said that we'd like a representative on the commission set up by the RFU to look at how rugby would change. Tony Hallett said we could have one, and then the RFU committee ignored it and didn't appoint anybody. We don't want to break away but we want to be involved in the decision-making process: the way competitions are run, players are registered, and contractual negotiations for television and sponsorship. We produced our own report that we gave to the commission, because we believed that theirs didn't fully cover what we recommended. The bottom line is that unless we get television revenue from the RFU, we won't be able to sign players at Gloucester when the moratorium is lifted on 4 May. We tried to be conciliatory and not aggressive, but without the money, the likely scenario is a breakaway.

Coley wasn't the only man who was concerned. Peter Wheeler, chief executive at Leicester, warned of most of England's brightest talents disappearing to the Southern

No way through: Ian Smith tries to break through the Sale defence.

Hemisphere to play, where the game was properly funded, and Donald Kerr, Harlequins representative, reiterated that clubs were fighting for their very future. Another to wade in with his two-penny worth was Fran Cotton, the former England international. Just as Tony Hallett saw the need for a European club competition, Cotton envisaged entrepreneurs propping rugby up.

One solution is that clubs look for a sugar daddy, someone who can put in money in the short term, because very few people in rugby clubs have any concept of how to run a professional sports business. Some sensible rules and regulations need to be put in place fast, because it's inevitable that people will be scrambling around for some short-term gain. The top part of the game needs to be controlled and managed by the Rugby Union, and we need a strategy for four or five years as to where they are going to take it. We want to compete at the highest level internationally, and there has to be a structure to allow this to happen.

As the league season drew to a close, EFDR's battle with the Union was reaching fever pitch, much like Gloucester's season on the field. They even got to the stage of asking the president, Bill Bishop, to help sort out the log jam EFDR saw as being created by Cliff Brittle, the RFU chairman. They had formulated a plan for a twelve-club top division, with a season that made sense from a rugby and commercial viewpoint, and were heartened by discussions with potential sponsors. The concept of up to fifteen home games per club, with cup competitions on top of the league structure, was put to the Union in the knowledge that they were bringing new money to the table.

As it transpired, the two parties didn't reach full agreement until after the following season had started, and clubs who had brought in backers – for example Bath (Andrew Brownsword), Newcastle (Sir John Hall), Richmond (Ashley Levitt) and Saracens (Nigel Wray) – had mopped up the top stars. Gloucester and Mike Coley, meanwhile, had gone their separate ways, and the Cherry & Whites had come out of the moratorium with only a handful of players on full-time contracts, and had been forced to concentrate their recruitment on young English players, among them Phil Vickery, Chris Catling, and Ed Pearce. The man who had adopted this policy was Gloucester's first director of rugby in the professional era.

COMINGS AND
GOINGS

Time to go – at least in Gloucester time.

Y ou've no doubt seen the car stickers. 'Young farmers do it in wellies' and others in the same vein. The favourite Gloucester one tends to be 'Can you survive The Shed?' but another, equally relevant, could be 'Gloucester do it in February'. Part company with their directors of rugby, that is. In fact, Nigel Melville ought to watch the post carefully in the second month of 2004. If a P45 is going to arrive, that historically is the most likely month of the year for it to do so.

It's baffling to understand why this should be. In amateur times, the old gag was that the coach was the thing used to transport players to away games. Many former players helped take Tuesday and Thursday evening training sessions at Kingsholm without the grand tag of being called a coach. However the greater demand for results, and time lying heavily on committee members' or board directors' hands once the Five (and subsequently Six) Nations start each spring may have had something to do with it.

The trend began in 1995. The author had just accepted a full-time post at BBC Radio Gloucestershire, but wasn't yet on the payroll. Ironically, the side had just beaten Leicester 9-3 on a muddy Kingsholm Saturday when Barrie Corless left, and the manner of his departure came as a surprise to Corless himself.

The chairman, Peter Ford, was ill at the time. He was away from both his business and the club. He had a problem with a clot in his neck and as I remember there was talk of quite a serious operation. I know he'd gone on a cruise, and three or four of the committee came in one afternoon, said they wanted a chat, and then told me they'd decided Gloucester didn't need a director of rugby anymore, and that was it. My mind went back to a conversation I'd had with Peter the previous summer, when he said 'watch your back – there are a lot of people at the club who would love to be doing what you are doing, and people who you think are your friends are not always your friends.' They had it all planned out, and what annoyed me was the person who was firing the bullets wasn't Alan Brinn, who was chairman in Peter's absence, but Fred Reed, who I had played squash with on a fairly regular basis. Perhaps he didn't like the fact that I used to beat him.

Gloucester had six League matches left that season when Corless' twenty-month stint at Kingsholm was ended. Viv Wooley, another former player who had come back to the club after coaching at Gloucester Old Boys, was placed in temporary charge, a more traditional move according to fans who felt Gloucester still showed a wariness of outsiders. Corless had strengthened the Under-21s (which Wooley had coached in Corless' first season) and the Colts, but most people don't look there for how the club is doing. They look, in the main, at the first XV results, and there had also been criticism over a lack of new players. Ultimately, as Alan Brinn recalls, the patience of the committee had run out.

It was desperately frustrating, because we had played some excellent rugby at times, but the problem was we were completely inconsistent. We did lose badly at Wasps and at Orrell, but we lost several games by only a few points, and we were hovering in and around the bottom four for most of the season. We couldn't keep going on like that. It wasn't good for anybody's heart. We had a reasonably talented squad, but we knew we lacked strength in depth in certain positions. We had good youngsters coming through but they take time to develop and in Division One you didn't have that time. We couldn't put a run of wins together. We set high standards at Gloucester and although we seemed to raise ourselves when we played Bath and Leicester, we tended to fade away against the others.

Fired up: Richard Hill on the touchline, flanked by Viv Wooley.

Sometimes coaches can buy themselves time if they've had a poor League season with a Cup run.

The prospect of some silverware from just a couple of results can paper over the cracks, at least in the interim. Barrie Corless didn't have that luxury, but Richard Hill could still have taken Gloucester to Twickenham in 1999. Gloucester had reached the quarter-finals of the Pilkington Cup by beating Worcester and Henley, and they had home advantage to come in the last eight against Harlequins when, almost four years to the day after Corless left Kingsholm, Hill also cleared his desk. He had been appointed in the autumn of 1995, once the professionalism issue had gone into overdrive. Initially he had been part-time, but he'd been full-time since the summer of 1996. Alan Brinn was still rugby club chairman, but under the new structure, it was David Foyle, chairman of Gloucester's board of directors, who went to see Hill at a Monday night training session. Not surprisingly, Hill clearly remembers events on that February evening.

David spoke to me and said that Gloucester rugby club was severing the contract based on Gloucester's league position. I couldn't really argue with that, even though the contract still had just over two years to run. We had hoped to be in the top five, and we were in the bottom five. Having said that, I had had no indication prior to that night as to what was going on. The squad needed to improve and there was a lot of hard work going in. Little things had decided some games but in professional sport the line between success and failure is very thin.

David Foyle, chairman of
Gloucester's board of directors.

Gloucester had lost to Harlequins in the League the previous Saturday, so on the face of it that was the straw that broke the camel's back for Richard Hill. It transpired, however, that the decision had been taken the previous Thursday. We'll never know what would have happened had Gloucester won at Kingsholm 48 hours later, but David Foyle felt the club couldn't wait any longer to make a change.

Since Christmas the results had been progressively worse, and the body language of the players on and off the pitch spoke volumes. We were grateful for what Richard had done for us but he seemed to have hit a brick wall. We set out clear objectives, and we'd set a budget to let him have the players he wanted to help the club achieve that objective. We were a poor tenth and that wasn't good enough. It was a commercial decision because we had put the admission prices up considerably at the start of the 1998/99 season and the fans hadn't been getting the rugby they expected. It would have been easy to have said that 'there's always next year' but we felt we should have taken a big stride forward.

Hill's right-hand man at Kingsholm was John Fidler, the former England lock forward who had combined running his construction business with the job of team manager. He had been called to a meeting on that Monday evening to be told of the departure of Hill, and no-one wanted the club to be successful more than the man known as 'Big Fids' ever since his son Rob progressed into the first XV.

The set up was very much as Richard wanted it. We had a squad of about thirty-six players, which was a lot, but he felt we needed a large squad. I always want the club to be successful, but at the time the product was too expensive for the money we were taking on the gate, and we had a lot of decisions to make. The brief from the Board was to get the squad down to the sort of numbers used by other clubs, which was twenty-six or twenty-eight. That was the harsh reality.

The man to tackle that thorny problem, along with Fidler, was Philippe Saint-André. While Australian centre Richard Tombs had become the first-ever overseas player to captain Gloucester, it was the former French captain who was to be the Cherry & Whites first foreign coach – and player/coach at that, at least initially. Hill had actually signed Saint-André as Gloucester embraced the professional era, so his excitement at being asked to succeed Hill was tempered with disappointment.

I was surprised and sad for Richard. We had a lot of injuries, and five or six players were out for five or six months, and Gloucester need a good team because a lot of people come and watch the games. The directors asked me if I wanted to take the squad for the rest of that season and prepare the squad for the next season. I thought we must play a lot more collective rugby, and that we must change the preparation. The training needed to be shorter and faster. To work the guys for four hours each day if the pitch was heavy was too much. We would play well for 50 minutes and then have problems in the last 30. We were fit but not fit to play rugby. We played some good games at home, but not away. The balance in the squad needed to be better. I had a lot of ideas in my mind.

Those ideas saw Saint-André steer Gloucester to a narrow Cup quarter-final win over Harlequins, although ultimately not as far as Twickenham. The Bath monkey was to

Time to start work: Philippe Saint-André (front) on his first day as director of rugby. (www.gpaimages.com)

remain for a while longer, although he did enjoy success in the short-lived Cheltenham and Gloucester Trophy, Gloucester retaining it by beating Bedford – as they had done in its inaugural season under Hill. Saint-André hung up his playing boots in the summer of 1999 to concentrate on running the team, which was a big enough job in itself, but the February factor was to come into play again in deciding Gloucester's latest change of playing management.

In December 1999, Philippe had agreed a contract through until the summer of 2002, but by Christmas 2001 discussions had already started about what would happen beyond that date. He'd been quite public about his position, saying that if the club wanted him to stay, he would consider the options that were presented to him. He was far more open and up front than others might have been. The clear impression was there were terms he would expect to be met, and if they weren't he might well go and do something else. Yet again, the decision to part company with a director of rugby put the spotlight on a game against Harlequins. It was announced that Saint-André's contract wasn't being renewed, and that he would leave the club after the Premiership match at the Stoop.

I have a lot of respect for Gloucester. The supporters were marvellous to me for five years. It was hard and there were a lot of rumours but that's life. I tried all the time to give my best and I am proud of what I did, especially in the last two years. In my career I played with my heart, and I think it's a value Gloucester supporters like. When I first took the team we lost away at West Hartlepool and Bedford, and the players weren't at the right level. My first job was to win, and that's what I tried to put into the minds of the players. The club had to think about the future and I understood that. In professional rugby you must anticipate.

It is fair to say life was never dull at Kingsholm under Philippe. For a player of such flair, particularly a Frenchman, to follow a tenacious, gritty England scrum half as Gloucester's playing supremo, contrasts in style were inevitable, but the yardstick is always the same – consistent results on the field. Former full-back Peter Butler, still the club's record point scorer, sees Saint-André's reign as a roller coaster.

The results hadn't been what the club demands. We may have been up there with the best of the rest, but we were still way behind the real best, which was Leicester. The money had been put in to warrant us being up alongside them. Philippe achieved passion for the club, but it was up and down. There were stories, things were happening in the background. The departure of Andy Keast

Points machine: former full-back Peter Butler scored 2,961 points for Gloucester between 1972 and 1982.

was a prime example. He was brought in and yet was gone in a few months. It seemed he couldn't settle. The negotiations were quite protracted too and I think that had an impact on the players.

Saint-André waved an emotional goodbye at the Stoop to hundreds of travelling Gloucester supporters, many of whom stayed on at the final whistle to wait for him at the end of the players' tunnel. From that day, his successor could only blow a promising position. The team were well placed to qualify for the 2002/03 Heineken Cup, and there was the prospect of a place in the end of season play-offs, which were in place for the first time. Paul Turner, the last backs coach employed by Saint-André, and an experienced operator in his own right, could have been appointed in a Viv Wooley-type 'caretaker' capacity, but owner Tom Walkinshaw didn't want to wait. Moreover, he knew the man he wanted to bring in.

I spoke to Nigel Melville in the latter part of 2001 when there was a lot of speculation that he would leave Wasps, and I said if he ever chose to leave, I'd be interested in having a chat. When

Leaving the nest: Nigel Melville in his time with Wasps, at Loftus Road. (www.gpaimages.com)

there was speculation he WOULD leave, I asked Wasps if we could make an approach, and they said we could. I saw him as one of the top coaches in the country, and thought he would bring an extra dimension to the club.

All this wasn't the best news for Turner, but he was astute enough to see the arguments. Some players had contracts that were up, and understandably they needed to know where they stood. There was also some recruitment to be done, and time was of the essence. Even allowing for the fact that Wasps wouldn't allow Melville to get fully involved until after the clubs had played each other in their outstanding Premiership fixture – something both parties accepted – Melville, like Richard Hill, another former England number 9, couldn't wait to get started. He agreed a four-year deal, and another former Gloucester legend, Mike Burton, felt it was a good appointment.

You have to remember Nigel managed the England Under-21s, and he had done a great job at Wasps. He's ideally equipped and he's a productive and constructive coach, but in the long term whether he is successful or not will be decided by the League standings. The crowd are knowledgeable and will give him a fair chance, and once you've proved you're not a 'jacker' to them, you're OK. Now he's here I hope he's right for the mix. He's a man of integrity, and you have to remember this is still one of the plum jobs. We have no League football here.

It was a view that was widely held. Nigel Melville had won a League championship and two domestic Cup finals at Twickenham with Wasps, where they had a reputation for having a very strong pack and a decent set of three quarters, a style Gloucester supporters would be very happy to accept in a winning formula. The impression was that within the current squad there was more that could be brought out. The Otley-born Melville, who followed his father Harry in playing for the town's rugby club, was the man charged with producing it.

UPHILL STRUGGLES

CLASSIC MATCH 3

10 April 1996, Kingsholm, Courage League
Gloucester 16 Bath 10

Gloucester turned Bath's world upside down with a memorable victory that ended their six-year domination of matches between the two clubs. The result, in a key Courage League fixture, leaves Gloucester needing just one more win to avoid relegation. The victory, achieved without seven first-choice players because of injury, was down to sheer commitment. Bath had the upper hand in both the scrums and the line-outs, but Gloucester soaked up almost everything they had to offer, and were kept in front by the goal kicking of full-back Tim Smith.

Watched by a crowd of over 10,000 – the biggest crowd at Kingsholm for four years – Gloucester made a dream start, scoring a try within four minutes. Bath infringed at a scrum on the halfway line, and Scott Benton tapped and ran immediately. He side-stepped his way at pace through the Bath defence, and when he was finally caught just short of the line, found wing Paul Holford on his shoulder. Holford dived over in the corner and Tim Smith converted from the touchline. Gloucester had given Bath too much respect in their cup semi-final three weeks earlier and they weren't going to make the same mistake twice. Bath full-back Audley Lumsden (who later had a spell at Gloucester) tried to kick from the wrong place after calling for a mark, and when the visitors collapsed the resultant scrum, Tim Smith added a penalty from in front of the posts, and they had a 10-0 lead. The danger then was the Bath response. Gloucester were forced to concede a string of penalties in the remainder of the first half, the bulk of which was Bath on the attack. Fly-half Richard Butland missed two penalties, but finally kicked one after Gloucester were penalised at a rolling maul, and apart from one dangerous charging run by Ben Clarke, Gloucester's tackling looked secure enough to contain the league leaders.

The early stages of the second half were intense, as both teams missed penalty chances to improve their position. Butland, who had a miserable night, squandered the opportunity to make it 10-6, while Gloucester were awarded three kickable goals as Bath's errors were penalised. All three chances for Smith were difficult, and all three were missed, but he made amends after being taken out high and late by Adedayo Adebayo. Gloucester now had a 10-point cushion, but as Ben Clarke limped off with 14 minutes left, the league leaders responded with a try. Gloucester lost a line-out on their own ball, and Bath spun it left to put centre Phil de Glanville in under the posts, Butland converting. It was again left to Smith to ease the nerves, kicking his third penalty of the night, Bath being penalised after a Butland clearance kick was charged down. Bath threw everything they had at Gloucester in the closing minutes, but the home defence stayed strong, even when Tim Smith fumbled a bouncing ball under pressure. The time-keeper's claxon signalled a jubilant pitch invasion from a crowd that had cheered and chanted throughout the match.

While the political wrangling was going on in the corridors of power at the RFU, with the Union and EFDR on opposite sides, a more localised battle was ensuing at the Recreation Ground, home of Bath. It was a battle that was to benefit Gloucester. The two men involved were both former England internationals, flanker John Hall and scrum-half Richard Hill, both key men in the successful Jack Rowell era. Ultimately Hall won out, and Hill was given the cold shoulder. As we now know, Hill joined Gloucester in September 1995, but as chairman Alan Brinn explains it might have happened even earlier.

Action man: Richard Hill in his playing days at Bath (OPPOSITE BELOW) and training with his new squad at Kingsholm (RIGHT).

We put out feelers out for Richard when he was still involved at Bath and we didn't have a director of rugby but those discussions didn't come to anything. When we went back a second time, it was Mike Teague who was instrumental in making contact with Richard. It was logical bearing in mind their time with England together. The initial idea was that he would come up and do a couple of sessions, but Mike soon thought we could get him on a more permanent basis. I remember meeting Mike one Monday night, and by the Wednesday Richard was on board part-time. He still had a job as a financial consultant and he had commitments outside the Courage League with England A, but we were delighted to have him, as we thought his ten years experience at Bath would strengthen the whole set-up.

Hill, as others will show later, was very much 'what you see is what you get'. He was thorough in his preparation and analysis, fully committed on the training ground, and whether Gloucester won or lost, he was always publicly supportive of his players as a group. Indeed, being appointed with the 120-day registration period in force for new players, he knew he had little option but to stabilise and improve the squad he inherited.

My job was to get the best out of each player. I knew a lot of them having played against them and seen them briefly in training. They all had certain strengths and we had to work out a strategy to get the best out of them. The attitude was second to none, but I knew I couldn't work wonders overnight. I wanted to pass on the latest methods from the England A set-up to help Viv Wooley with the coaching, and assess the fitness and skill levels, which I thought had risen generally in the game by 40 per cent in five years. If Gloucester were to compete with Bath, we had to look at personal training programmes and individual skills, but I didn't want to come in and be seen as a dictator. I wanted to earn the players' respect, by introducing ideas and getting them to see they were helping. I even thought a different attitude might improve their performance by 20 per cent.

Hill's appointment was confirmed, ironically, after a 37–11 defeat at the Rec by Bath. His first official match in charge was at Orrell on 7 October, a match Gloucester lost, and a match skipper Dave Sims remembers for an outburst by a supporter.

I always felt I was given 100 per cent support by the fans even when the team was suffering, but after that game we were walking back to get some beer for the bus and this fan had a real go, abusing me, the works. I couldn't believe it.

It was to be a long time before Hill sampled his first competitive Gloucester win. A promising position at Saracens slipped through their fingers when Andy Lee kicked a late penalty in the days when they still played at Southgate, and there were other away defeats at Sale and Bristol. With Leicester, Harlequins and Wasps winning at Kingsholm, Hill had presided over six straight league defeats. The turn of the year arrived with Gloucester still in the Pilkington Cup after beating national league side Walsall, but with just one league win to their name. Hill was struggling to make an impact in terms of results, and it took a stroke of fortune to lend him a helping hand. West Hartlepool, also struggling near the foot of the table, came to Kingsholm on 6 January 1996. This was a match Gloucester dare not lose, or they would be staring fairly and squarely at the prospect of relegation with no obvious improvement in sight and games running out. 17–11 ahead with time almost up, West's full-back Tim Stimpson out-manoeuvred Tom Beim, who was filling in for the injured Tim Smith at full back. He got round close to the posts before touching the ball down. The lead was now only 17–16, with an easy conversion to come. Few could believe what happened after that. Stimpson, almost in line with the one upright, barely fifteen metres out, slid his kick past rather than through the posts. The referee blew for full time. Gloucester had had an amazing escape, and Richard Hill knew it.

I couldn't watch Stimpson's kick. It was the Saracens away game all over again, and I was really concerned about what I was going to say to the players, but I heard the roar when he missed it. Little things weren't going right for us and we all needed a bit of luck. We had no-one to kick any goals when Tim Smith went off and Tom Beim wasn't in the right position when Stimpson scored his try. West's running lines were good and our three quarters looked worried. We were workmanlike but we didn't have a lot of pace, and there's no substitute for that. We'd actually played better in other games and lost, but that was a turning point.

The 1995/96 season was a curious affair. Ten league games on consecutive Saturdays until 11 November, and then just two until the end of the March, when Gloucester's last six fixtures were to determine their survival. Hindsight says the fixture list gave Hill too little time at the start to get Gloucester into a safe position, and losing that game to West Hartlepool might have seen him go the same way as Barrie Corless. That result, however, bought him some breathing space, and a vital home win over Orrell set up a cliff hanger

Escape: Adey Powels and Pete Miles commiserate with West Hartlepool full-back Tim Stimpson.

of a finale at the end of the season, a spell that contained two of Gloucester's most memorable wins in recent years.

The Cherry & Whites arrived at the season's finishing straight having just been knocked out of the cup in the semi-finals. Three of their remaining six games were away, while old rivals Bristol and fellow strugglers Saracens still had to visit Kingsholm. It was however, the visit of Bath that really lit the blue touch paper. Predictably, the away game at Wasps had been lost, but Mark Mapletoft had just kicked Gloucester to victory over Bristol the previous Saturday. The Bath game not only brought Richard Hill and his old club into opposition for the first time in a league fixture, it also gave the Cherry & Whites the chance to avenge that cup semi-final defeat less than three weeks earlier – and, the game was midweek. Kingsholm under lights is an even more inspiring venue than normal.

To a man, all the players who are featured later in the '100 club' (only Terry Fanolua wasn't at Gloucester at the time) remember it as one of their major highlights. Paul Holford's early try after a break by Scott Benton was converted by Tim Smith, who was to add three penalties later on as Gloucester retained the lead throughout, despite Bath's lofty league position and star-studded team. Lock Pete Miles was one of the heroes.

We were possibly expected to lose but Richard (Hill) said to just go out and enjoy ourselves and give the people something to shout about. The crowd carried us through. They shaded the line-outs but we tackled everything that moved. It was the best win of my life.

Hill felt tactically he had got it right on the night.

The performances of Scott Benton and Martyn Kimber were the key. We battled for everything and when we did get the ball the half backs played it beautifully. We kept it simple, drilled it into the corners and let Bath make the mistakes. We started as if we meant it. We had been too tense the previous Saturday and I said to play with smiles on our faces, and actually we made very few errors and defensively we were very good. If someone had asked me at the start of the season which game I wanted to win most, it would have been beating Bath at Kingsholm. Very few sides will beat Gloucester at home when it's heaving like that. I was getting carried away and I wasn't even playing.

That 16-10 win opened the door to possible escape. The RFU and the clubs organisation, EFDR, were still arguing over relegation, but it looked, if results went to form, like the winner of the final match of the season against Saracens at Kingsholm would remain in the top flight, while the loser would go down in the second relegation place. West Hartlepool was already well adrift.

So it was that on a warm sunny day, 27 April 1996, Kingsholm staged a shoot out to stay up, or so we thought. A fortnight after the end of the season, the decision was taken that there would be no relegation, and that the league would be extended to twelve teams with the promotion of London Irish and Northampton. On the day however, nobody knew that would be the outcome. Gloucester and Saracens both began the match with ten points, although the Cherry & Whites had a considerable advantage in terms of their point difference. Rarely can Kingsholm have found its collective voice as loudly as when Tony Windo somehow found his way over the try line from close range in the first half, but as Richard Hill remembers, they'd been stoked up from well before the game actually started.

We were in the dressing room before the Bath match, and on the spur of the moment I sent all the players out for a jog round. They got a huge lift from the reception, so we thought we'd do it again. I think them running in front of the Shed probably put the fear of God into Saracens.

Having established a 14-3 half-time lead, Gloucester started running down the clock well before the end, and even a late try converted by Matt Singer still left Saracens needing two scores. They didn't get either. The one disappointment, from a sentimental point of view, was the omission of Tim Smith from the Gloucester side. After announcing he was to retire, Smith was left on the bench, one appearance short of 350 for the club.

Every dog has his day, and it was time to go before the professional era came in. A lot of players had come and gone – Blakeway, Boyle, Gadd, Teague and Longstaff, Richard Mogg and Paul Taylor – I may have missed the boat as regards money but there would have been no way I'd have given up what I had. I used to watch the odd big game with my father, and then I was playing alongside a few of the ones I used to watch. There were so many highlights – the cup wins at Wasps and Northampton in 1990, and the win over Bath under lights stand out. A lot of people refer to Twickenham as HQ, but Kingsholm was HQ to me.

Famous win: Paul Holford escapes the Bath defence to score an early try (ABOVE). Mike Teague and
Viv Wooley in front of an elated crowd at the final whistle (BELOW).

Unbearable: Tim Smith in the dug-out, unable to watch.

Hill's reaction to the win and the season's outcome was suitably circumspect.

I was pleased with the turnaround in the second half of the season, but all we did was escape relegation. When you are second from bottom you can't experiment, because you're fighting for every bit of possession, let alone every point. If we had gone down it would have been a hard road back. People knew my policy. I didn't want to disrupt the spirit or the balance, but I wanted young players who knew what the club was about. Players with potential like Scott Benton. There was a growing market for players because money was becoming important, but both Dave Sims and Phil Greening had offers to go elsewhere and stayed put. I used to think Gloucester had a higher price in that way than any other club, because playing at Gloucester meant so much more.

Hill's relief was mirrored by chairman Alan Brinn.

Richard was so honest and so passionate that he soon got the respect of the players and everyone else at the club. Barrie Corless once said to me 'my job is impossible because you are an unfashionable club'. I was stunned by that. It wasn't 'we' but 'you'. Richard said 'we' are going to try and make this the best club in the country. We approached him about going full time and he was delighted to do so. We wanted to fulfil that potential.

Hill's structure for doing so was the most extensive ever at Kingsholm. He employed a psychologist, Jack Lamport-Mitchell, and a specialist fitness advisor, Joseph Picken. Mike Rafter was brought in as forwards coach, with Viv Wooley asked to take on the United forwards. There would be a new development XV, replacing the disbanded

Under-21s, and Nick Marment and Pat Keily, who now eight years on, is coach at Lydney, would guide the Colts. The club were allowed fifty registered players, and there were a raft of new young faces that summer, but as early as mid-October the development XV was disbanded. Hill felt Gloucester were leading the way in taking the decision.

Rugby was going through massive changes, even week to week. It was essential we had a good youth set-up but we had one tier too many. A natural split was emerging – those who could train during the day, and those who were in full-time employment or education. It had looked the right structure at the start of the season, but we were learning all the time and I soon felt we didn't need four teams.

Little was Hill to know at that stage how the season would pan out. His infamous statement about targeting matches came unstuck immediately as Gloucester conceded eleven tries and seventy-five points in their opening game at Harlequins. They didn't get another such pasting until the penultimate league match at Bath. It took a month – and four more league defeats – to steady things before a home win over Wasps, and by then the league table was starting to split.

Windo of opportunity: prop Tony Windo burrows his way over for a vital try against Saracens.

Clean sheet: Simon Devereux breaking in Gloucester's 30-0 win over Orrell.

Gloucester, London Irish, Orrell and West Hartlepool were filling the bottom four places, and the quartet were in danger of becoming detached. Fortunately, Hill had key positions in the team settled – the front five (Windo, Greening, Deacon, Fidler and Sims), the half backs (Benton and Mapletoft) and the full back (Catling), and the fixture list gave Gloucester six consecutive matches against the strugglers. Doubles were done home and away against all three, and with a quarter-final spot in the cup already secured, Richard Hill knew by early February that Gloucester's nerves shouldn't be shredded by another tense finale.

I had a chart in my office. On 11 January we had eight points, and I believed we needed eighteen to stay up. By that stage we had won seven games on the trot (fourteen points), and we still had ten games to play. The Orrell game was hard to watch because there were too many handling errors, but we'd done what was required in the relegation battle and I wanted us to try and pick off sides above us.

The cup semi-final against Leicester will be dealt with below, but in the wonderful way that sport has, Gloucester were again to be pitted against their cup opponents in the league at Kingsholm a short time later. It had happened 12 months earlier when Bath, despite being beaten, held their nerve to take the championship. The Tigers weren't so lucky. 8 April 1997 is a date etched on the memory of Gloucester supporters, not just because of the result, but the way in which it was achieved, and because the match was watched by a distinguished guest. Several supporters spotted Philippe Saint-André at the ground to watch one of the finest matches Kingsholm has ever seen. The lead bounced back and forth until well into injury time, when Gloucester, trailing 30-25, won a line-

Night-time magic: scrum-half Scott Benton at close quarters against Leicester [RIGHT] and the team celebrating their 32-30 win over the Tigers [BELOW].

out and drove towards the Leicester line. The forwards piled over, the try was awarded and Mark Mapletoft kicked the winning conversion. I vividly remember Dean Richards' solemn face as he walked down the tunnel at the end, Leicester's title hopes in tatters. It was the second time Gloucester had avenged a cup semi-final result with a crucial home league victory, and Mapletoft finished a mixed night with his kicks on a high note.

I would have been gutted had we lost as I was disappointed with my first couple of kicks. I hadn't had many kicks to win games then and there was a delay while Rob (Fidler) was down injured. I just tried to strike it as well as possible. I remember for the first five or ten minutes we couldn't get in the game but the crowd pulled us along and the front eight gave everything. We just tried to support them as much as we could. It was a brilliant night.

Gloucester's season had been one of steady improvement after that bad start. They had won eleven and drawn one of their last seventeen league matches, and reached the last four of the Pilkington Cup, but off the field the club was about to be brought into line with the likes of Bath and Saracens, and the promoted clubs, Bedford, Newcastle and Richmond. A year earlier Gloucester had reported a loss of £140,000, and had formed a Board of Directors to help steer the club into the professional era. The chairman of the Board was David Foyle.

A packed EGM listens as David Foyle addresses the members.

If we were going to keep our better players, and attract new ones, it was going to need a massive injection of money. We had again survived on a budget loss, but another one for the following season was unacceptable. Various people had advised us through that season on investing in the club. We'd tried to look at every option but we couldn't raise enough money. As a board we didn't need the members' approval through an EGM but it would have been unwise not to ask them, because such a move was likely to involve about 75 per cent of the club's shares being sold.

Some of the key players, such as hooker Phil Greening, also felt something had to be done.

We survived on true grit. There was about five of us that wanted to stay but we wanted the club to show some ambition. It wasn't an ultimatum but we wanted to be playing in the big games and competing in Europe so we wanted the members to endorse the Board's view. If the members hadn't backed the idea of a backer, I think we'd have gone down the following year. We wouldn't have been able to compete.

Enter Tom Walkinshaw.

MOVING
WITH THE
TIMES

CLASSIC MATCH 4

23 August 1997, Kingsholm, Allied Dunbar Premiership
Gloucester 35   Bristol 13

Gloucester's Premiership season exploded into life in the second half as they comprehensively defeated old rivals Bristol. It took Gloucester a full 40 minutes to get going, but after trailing 6-0 at half-time, they made up for it after the break by scoring four tries. The match was notable for the debuts of all four players in Gloucester's star studded back line – Philippe Saint-André, his brother Raphael, Richard Tombs and Terry Fanolua.

Director of coaching Richard Hill had impressed on his players the need to dominate Bristol through the pack and not be tempted to run every scrap of possession, but the instructions went out of the window in the first half. Gloucester were swamped by nerves, and the line-out functioned so badly that hooker Phil Greening was replaced at half-time by another debutant, Neil McCarthy. Gloucester did turn over some possession in the mauls but it hardly made up for the lack of clean first-phase ball. Apart from one individual run by Raphael Saint-André which resulted in a try being disallowed, the only points worthy of note in the first half were two early Bristol penalties, both kicked by Paul Burke, and one missed chance for fly-half Mark Mapletoft.

Whatever Richard Hill said at half-time, he made good use of the new ten-minute interval, much to the delight of new backer Tom Walkinshaw, who had flown in from watching his Arrows Formula 1 team in qualifying for the Belgian Grand Prix. McCarthy's role at the line-out was faultless, and from there everything else clicked into place as the pack got their act together and at last gave the backs a real chance. Within two minutes they had sucked in the Bristol defence, developed the attack around the fringes, and then spread the ball to give Philippe Saint-André his first scoring chance. He sprinted over the line wide on the left, and although Mapletoft couldn't convert, Gloucester were up and running.

Mapletoft soon added a penalty to put Gloucester ahead for the first time, and the crowd was brought to its feet by a spectacular score. Winning the ball on their own 22, Gloucester attacked. Tombs fed Fanolua and his break set Saint-André in for his second try of the match, this time under the posts, making the conversion easy for Mapletoft. Bristol's response was hampered by Eben Rollitt's yellow card, but they did manage a try by David Corkery, converted by Burke, midway through the second half.

At 18-13 the score suggested the match was in the balance, but it was Gloucester who pulled away. Prop Tony Windo charged over the line after skipper Pete Glanville was held up just short, Mapletoft converting, and then the fly half kicked his third penalty of the match after strong breaks by Deacon and Philippe Saint-André had created pressure on the Bristol defence. Rob Fidler's try beside the posts in the last minute, again converted by Mapletoft, rounded off a second half that had been in stark contrast to the first.

Four months of negotiation culminated in Tom Walkinshaw being unveiled as Gloucester's new owner on 29 April 1997. The fifty-year-old son of a Lanarkshire farmer had bought a 73 per cent stake in the club, despite a background of more than twenty years as a driver, designer and team manager in motor sport. He was also, at the time, known for being the man to attract former world Formula 1 champion Damon Hill to his Arrows team. Now he had another Hill in his portfolio.

All this seemed a million miles from twelve months earlier when David Foyle, then elected chairman of the new Board of Directors, had announced a new sponsorship deal between the club and Westbury Homes. At that stage he said he couldn't see the club accepting one man doing what he liked with Kingsholm. A year on, he accepted the change was inevitable.

We asked ourselves one simple question – do we want Kingsholm to have First Division rugby? If the answer was yes, we had to go down this route. With no backer, we would have been resigned to losing our best players and then risk sliding into the second division, and who knows what would have happened after that. My grandfather was on the Gloucester committee in 1929 and I had served for ten years as membership secretary. I don't think any of the Board of Directors was quite sure what we were taking on at the start of the season, but the whole season was about breaking moulds. I'd met Tom about half a dozen times by then and each time I left with a buzz about what he could do for Gloucester.

Those feelings were echoed by club chairman Alan Brinn.

I didn't think we could have found a better person if we had to go down this route. It was amazing the interest he showed with all his other commitments and we had good vibes from him.

Walkinshaw himself said precisely what you would have expected.

When David approached me and asked if I was interested in helping Gloucester, I took the request very seriously. Gloucester is only 45 minutes away for me and it's a big challenge and a great honour to be part of this team. It's an exciting opportunity to try and help Gloucester reach their objective of being the top team in the country.

The move was a huge weight off the shoulders of director of rugby Richard Hill. Despite the advantage of one of the highest average gates in the Courage League, Hill had seen Harlequins, Bath and Saracens spend millions on their squads, while he had

Signing in: Tom Walkinshaw is
unveiled as Gloucester's backer.

one of the lowest playing budgets in the division. Now there was a balance to be redressed.

We needed to be able to recruit three or four international-class players, and to pay our own players a competitive salary. They weren't asking for £500,000 a year, just a fair return. I tried to promote young English players but you could go to Bath and Leicester and find a good player was on £80,000 a year, so to buy up a contract like that was a lot of money. It was my responsibility to build a successful side, because the players didn't want the anxiety of tottering on the verge of relegation. We didn't need to spend what the rest were spending, but if we wanted to compete with the top four we had to join them financially, and just be sensible about it.

The arrival of a backer, whoever it was to be, had looked an odds-on certainty from the previous week. The club had revealed the acquisition of Philippe Saint-André, the vastly experienced French wing, on a two-year deal, with an option for a further twelve months. Saint-André had followed fellow countrymen Thierry LaCroix, Laurent Cabannes and Philippe Sella to England, so it was no surprise that David Foyle revealed that the agreement with Tom Walkinshaw was tied up – but under wraps – when Saint-André signed. Not surprisingly, Richard Hill was delighted to have landed a world-class player and someone who had been a fine ambassador for French rugby.

Top men: Tom Walkinshaw and director of rugby Richard Hill.

He was the first player I looked at and I thought he'd be an ideal choice as Gloucester's first overseas player. Most of the foreign signings had been players who had come to the end of their international careers and been discarded by their country but Philippe was still in the French squad. He was a superb finisher, and very fair with the financial package. I felt he would pass on all his experience to our younger players.

It was useful that Hill could speak enough French to be able to communicate with Saint-André in his native tongue. His English was sketchy enough when he signed that he brought an interpreter with him, and some would argue that particularly when he succeeded Hill as director of rugby, the language barrier was a factor in his ability to communicate ideas. His greatest concern initially was to be able to help Gloucester's rising stars develop.

Gloucester have an impressive pack and some young and talented players in the backs. That's a good base. They have lots of enthusiasm, and that's why I wanted to join them. It's the first time an active international has come to England, but the French president and the coaches understand the position. It is a last chance for me to play rugby full time.

Saint-André would be part of a cosmopolitan back line once the new season started the following August, as Richard Hill recruited a Samoan and an Australian to join him, showing how global a job it had become to find new players. The pair turned into one of Gloucester's best centre partnerships of the professional era, Terry Fanolua and

First of the Foreign Legion: Philippe Saint-André signs for Gloucester and answers questions from the local and national media.

Richard Tombs providing a balance of guile and tenacity. The Hill jigsaw was slowly taking shape.

I remember getting Richard was a long process, as he was contracted to New South Wales and the Australian Rugby Union. He had five full caps, and he'd played about sixty state games for NSW. The Lions had done well on tour and English rugby had gained prestige. He wanted a new challenge and he saw the first division as an exciting one to play in. We saw Terry when the Samoans were in England the previous autumn. He'd played well when I saw him at Richmond and we tracked him through the Hong Kong Sevens. I eventually met him with the Samoan manager Brian Williams, who played on the wing for the All Blacks, and he seemed keen to come and play in England. I felt he had pace and good hands, but the biggest thing was his tackling. It was terrific. Once he'd hit you, you knew about it.

Their arrival was to kick start a long list of foreign players to move in and out of Kingsholm in the last six seasons. Italy, New Zealand and South Africa have been represented as well as Australia, France and Samoa, and I'm sure you have your favourites. In all, Hill released fourteen players in the summer of 1997, but one of his new stars, Philippe Saint-André, became an instant hit with two tries on his Premiership debut at home to Bristol, a major plus for the new owner.

The guys looked a bit jittery to begin with but they did really well in the second half. They've been very committed. We know there will be ups and downs but it's a long-term job to build the club up.

Ultimately, the season was one where Gloucester picked up their first piece of silverware for more than twenty years, and several players achieved notable personal milestones. Prop Phil Vickery won his first England cap, and Mark Mapletoft, having won his first (and only) cap against Argentina, scored over 400 points for the second season running.

Centre of attention: Richard Tombs (with ball) and Terry Fanolua on their league debut against Bristol.

Deadly: Philippe Saint-André marks his Gloucester debut by scoring against Bristol.

Terry Fanolua was named as player of the season in his first year at the club, and Gloucester recorded their highest-ever score and record-winning margin in the same match against Fylde.

That game was in the group stages of a new knockout competition, the Cheltenham & Gloucester Trophy. It was one belittled in some quarters but taken seriously by Gloucester once they had come through the group stages, which also involved games against West Hartlepool, Northampton and Wakefield. By this time Tom Walkinshaw had allowed Richard Hill to go over his playing budget to sign wing Brian Johnson and versatile England back-row Steve Ojomoh.

The Cherry & Whites then beat Richmond at home in the quarter-finals, an historic game as Richard Tombs became the first overseas player to skipper the Cherry & Whites, and then won 53-15 at Leicester in the last four, on the day Mark Mapletoft passed 1,000 points for the club. This set up a final against Bedford, but the fledgling status of the C&G Trophy was shown in that the final wasn't played at Twickenham, but at Franklins Gardens, Northampton – a neutral venue for the two clubs.

The match provided Pete Glanville with something to show for his year as captain. Gloucester scored first, and retained the lead throughout, outscoring Bedford by four tries to three. Mark Mapletoft's contribution to the 33-25 scoreline – a try, two conversions, two dropped goals and a penalty (18 points) – saw him voted Man of the Match, and Richard Hill felt this heralded the start of better things for his team.

When you win your first bit of silverware, it does give you the confidence to go on. The important thing once you've got to a final is to win it. We were under the cosh at times but when we got our chances we scored. I think we got into the Bedford 22 four times in the first half, and each time we got a score. That's very clinical.

Considering the changes in the playing staff it was perhaps disappointing that Gloucester's league record was identical in Walkinshaw's first season to the last the club went through without him. Eleven wins, one draw and ten defeats again saw a mid-table finish, with never any real threat of a challenge at the top or any worries over relegation. The point difference, though, was considerably better, just –16, compared to –113 the year before, and Walkinshaw reflected on a year where the graph of progress had been steadily rising.

This is a young team and it will continue to improve. Everyone has worked hard to re-establish the club and get the confidence back. We've had good support all season (although the crowds were well short of current levels) and it would be easy to pinpoint two or three games where we should have won but they slipped through our fingers. Our target was the top six, but we look capable to getting into the top five. Richard and I talk all the time and we are already planning for next season.

One of those key summer decisions involved a change of policy. Traditionally, the end of the season saw the squad photograph, to mark the players who had played the most matches the season before, and the choosing of the following season's captain in a players' vote. Richard Hill decided it was time for him to have a say as to who he wanted to lead the team, and though the players were asked, it was Hill who took the final decision. The captain's armband was to go back to Dave Sims.

For me, Dave was the ideal man. He would have been captain the year before but his wife had just had a baby. He and I worked well together. He was captain when I arrived and for the first two seasons there was tremendous pressure on him. We didn't have Tombs, Fanolua or Saint-André to help him, and he had two young half backs in Benton and Mapletoft. By the time he came back we had Ojomoh in the back row as well as other decision makers, so he could concentrate on motivating the team. He had a terrific attitude towards the club, and was an awesome sight if you saw him in the tunnel.

It's hard to know why Gloucester weren't able to go to the next level from what looked a good platform. Hill acquired Simon Mannix from Sale during the closed season, but the 1998/99 campaign was one of increasing frustration in the new-look Premiership, which had fourteen clubs rather than twelve. With no European matches to worry about, the league dominated the first half of the season. Gloucester were unlucky to lose Pete Glanville and Simon Devereux with long-term injuries, and when Hill tried to cover for them by signing Kingsley Jones from Ebbw Vale, he too was soon on the sidelines. The side won well against Richmond in their opening away Premiership fixture, but were singularly poor after that away from Kingsholm, and the midweek defeat at Harlequins set a sorry tone. The defeat at Wasps on 27 December 1998 was their fifth in a row away from home, although with Wasps only sneaking the points with two late tries, Richard Hill sensed an improvement might be around the corner.

That was the first game for a while where I'd seen an aggressive attitude – not nasty, just aggressive. Our tackle count in the second half was seventy-three. In the first half it was thirty-eight, but you can't expect to defend as much as that and get away with it. I don't want us to be an easy side to referee. I want us to be asking questions of him all the time. The forwards are doing well but our back line hasn't performed well this season, and we seem to have come to a bit of a plateau. It's a case of me now getting across to the players that we're going to have put in extra effort. We can't go along as we have done and it's going to take another big push.

It was fortunate that Gloucester were able to keep clear of any real trouble with six wins from their first seven home Premiership matches. Hopes of a happy new year prevailed after a win over Bath, but then Richmond rallied to draw at Kingsholm in between Pilkington Cup wins over two clubs from outside the top division, Worcester and Henley. A bad defeat at London Irish, and a home loss to Harlequins meant Gloucester had won only eight of twenty Premiership matches, and Richard Hill acknowledged there was a lot of work still to do.

Tradition maintained: Gloucester, winners of the Knockout Cup in its inaugural season, repeat the feat in the C&G Trophy. (Bruce Seabrook/www.gpaimages.com)

Time running out: A miserable Richard Hill at the home game against Harlequins.

Quins were fitter and stronger than us, and we do seem to struggle to keep pace with sides in the last twenty minutes. They looked more composed on the ball, and the try they scored just after half-time was a killer. We went off the boil when we were 10-0 up, conceded three penalties and suddenly it was 10-9. We had three good scoring chances within five metres of their line – two line-outs and a scrum – and we squandered all of them. The players tried hard but it's a big disappointment.

It was a result Hill wasn't allowed the chance to put right. As we have already seen, barely forty-eight hours later, the curse of the February sacking was to strike the former Bath and England scrum half. Now, more than four years on, and after spells at Harlequins and in Wales with Ebbw Vale and Newport, Hill is the man charged with bringing Bristol back into the top flight. Most supporters will wish him well, acknowledging that he had arguably the most turbulent phase in the history of the game to deal with in his time at Gloucester. His efforts were a huge factor in starting the process by which the club has reached its current status as one of England's representatives in the 2003/04 Heineken Cup, and one of the cornerstones around which Hill built that platform is still playing at the age of 38.

ANDY
DEACON

At the height of their success twenty years ago, Nottingham Forest Football Club had a left winger called John Robertson. He wasn't a natural athlete, and had no great pace. Forest manager Brian Clough described him as looking about as dangerous as an old lady on a push bike – probably one with a wicker basket on the front. You might say the same about a 38-year-old prop playing professional rugby in the top division of the English game. Actually, you'd be wrong. Spend any length of time in the company of Andy Deacon and his determination to be the best that he can be rubs off on you. He compares playing professional rugby to winning the pools, and his attitude is not to spend, spend, spend. He wants to make the most of every last drop of his good fortune.

Breaking through: 'Deacs' in 1992.

Deacon is the one man to experience the last thirteen years at Gloucester. In 1990 he was at Kingsholm, having gone there, like so many before him, from Longlevens. He was trying to establish himself in a strong United side, but hadn't done enough at that stage to make the end of season first XV squad photograph. That honour was still two years away. As he watched the cup final from the stands, little could he have realised that in 2003 he would be standing on the pitch at Twickenham with his son, Oliver, picking up Gloucester's first 'major' honour since 1978.

His love of rugby came from his days at Beaufort school in the city, where Andrew Deacon was very much an all rounder. He won colours at five different sports, as well as playing rugby for the school side, ultimately as a prop, though he did have a stint as a second row. His rugby master was John Simonett, a lean no. 8 at Kingsholm in the 1970s, and under his guidance, the youthful Deacon was part of the first team from Beaufort to beat a side from Sir Thomas Rich's Grammar School since Beaufort was opened. It had taken five years.

By the time he tried his luck at Gloucester, Deacon had married Karen, who he met as a teenager, and had built up some useful experience playing for the first XV at Longlevens, even though it meant a trek across the city from Tuffley to play. He made his debut against Spartans, a daunting task for anyone bearing in mind the rivalry in the city, but even more so for a 15-year-old schoolboy. He left Beaufort twelve months later, and was working for brewers Whitbread by the time he went to Kingsholm in 1987 – when life in the Deacon house followed a very strict pattern.

I used to get up at 5.30, get to work for 6, and then try and finish by 12 or 12.30. I'd go training in the afternoon, come home for a kip, and then train again in the evening. I'd do that every day, and that's how my life was for years. If we did play on a Wednesday, then I'd have a few beers afterwards, but the rest of the week was the same. It was gruelling and I was permanently tired. I was lucky that Karen was very understanding but I couldn't do it now. I was lucky I could train in the afternoon but I used to get annoyed if I got stuck on a job somewhere and couldn't get back.

That state of permanent fatigue was clearly felt by the first XV too as that 1990 Cup final approached. It is always difficult for sides which are competing for silverware on several fronts, and although for Gloucester it was only two, both came to a head only seven days apart. We will never know if a victory against Nottingham the previous week would have made for a closer final, or even been the first half of a Cup and League double, but Deacon was concerned, having trained against the players who were to represent Gloucester that day. There were a lot of niggling injuries, and the side was running out of steam. Some people were playing who really shouldn't have been playing, but the

Elation: Deacon with son, Oliver, lifting the Powergen Cup at Twickenham. (www.gpaimages.com)

selection committee went with the tried and tested, and on a hot day, the Gloucester team was caught out. It's an emotion Deacon remembers when comparing the 1990 final with the Powergen win over Northampton.

The Bath game was over long before the end, and when you're losing that's the worst feeling in the world, especially in front of a big crowd. I remember watching and thinking they were playing for ages before the final whistle went. This year against Northampton, I had the feeling we were going to win. We were playing our hearts out but we had the lead and our defence was holding up. We knew we could hold them and it's great when it's like that. People often ask me if it was planned that I would go and pick up the Cup, but we were all stood waiting to go up, and Jake Boer just turned to me and said to go and get it. It was as off the cuff as that.

Deacon's longevity at Kingsholm has seen him serve under a miscellany of staff. Former player Keith Richardson was coach to the first team when he first walked up the tunnel, and Nigel Melville is the fourth director of rugby, following Barrie Corless, Richard Hill and Philippe Saint-André. Interestingly, since Richardson's departure, all four have been backs, while all Gloucester's captains have been forwards, including Deacon himself. Stand off Mike Hamlin, skipper under Richardson, was the last back to lead the team. Deacon's one season in charge was 1994/95, a time of upheaval at the club, and not a time he remembers with any great fondness.

I was injured that year having broken my collar bone playing for Emerging England. The operation didn't go well and being captain, there was a pressure to play. I was out of sorts and out of form, and I played poorly. Mike Teague was an immense help to me but there were times where I should have said I wasn't fit and I wasn't going to play. It's nice now when people say nice things about you but I've got a long memory and people said a lot of **** when I was captain, and those people are still about.

Being a figure in the public eye isn't something that sits easily on Deacs' broad shoulders. He'd much rather keep a low profile. The adulation that followed the victory over the Saints meant that rather than just being stopped wherever he was by rugby folk who had known him for years, all and sundry wanted to talk. He could hardly go anywhere for a month without someone delaying him. That one game had catapulted him into the minds of people who had previously been gloriously unaware of Andy Deacon, yet he may never have got the opportunity.

The 2001/02 season was, on his own admission, one of Deacon's most frustrating at the club. He played only a handful of first-team matches, and that meant lots of training with no end product, some of it alone. It almost seemed like a penalty for not playing. He had to maintain his belief in his own ability – something he found hard at times – and be ready if the telephone rang on a Friday night or a Saturday morning to step up to the plate and perform, knowing that another chance may not come until weeks or even months later. Injuries though, can open doors, and props are more susceptible than most, and Deacon's patience was rewarded when Phil Vickery was sidelined with a back injury that needed an operation. Without that, Deacon probably wouldn't have played at Twickenham, and may again have watched his team mates from the stands.

If it's possible, Andy Deacon is enjoying his rugby now more than ever before, and you sense that is down to the people he is working with. Every coach will have their own ideas, every player will add something different, but the thought processes now are so open, that here is an old prop who is revelling in the situation he finds himself in.

*My memory of Keith Richardson is of someone who was trying to do things that had never been done before. Keith was an intelligent man and that was the way he coached. He did come back as forwards coach under Richard Hill but for whatever reason it didn't work out. In between Viv Wooley looked after the forwards under Barrie Corless, but we were only scraping by. In fact we'd been doing that for a while. We hoped things would get better without really having any evidence that they would. There was no plan to make them get better. I admired Richard Hill a lot. He coached like he played. He was gritty, and because we were all professional by then, he'd have us in at nine, and we'd train twice a day until five. He wanted to use all the available time, and compared to today he had no backup at all. I felt the club kicked him in the teeth a bit but I wasn't involved in the decision. Philippe was the complete opposite. Short sessions and no organisation. Nigel Melville and Dean Ryan are different again, and Dean is the best forwards coach I've ever worked with. I'm doing drills now I've never done before, and I thought I'd seen them all. I don't know where he gets them from, but he's very good at breaking the game right down and the more technical it gets, the more switched on you have to be. Our game sheets are written up as a team, and he'll get one of us to go through them with a flip chart and a video. Initially the guys would take the **** until they realised it could be them next. They've created an environment where you have to be on the button all the time, and it's clever because there have been very few moans about selection, and that's saying something when you're trying to keep thirty-odd blokes happy.*

In the fullness of time, Deacon may be bracketed with other Gloucester players who were highly regarded but never capped by their country. Mickey Booth, a veteran of over 400 games for the Cherry & Whites as a scrum half, and Richard Mogg, who scored the

Innovative: Deacon's first coach at Gloucester, Keith Richardson.

winning try in the 1978 final against Leicester, and who passed 500 matches by the time he played in the 1990 final, would be just two examples. Deacon though, will stand alone in one regard. He was the first player to be granted a testimonial by the club, in recognition of his long service.

The decision was taken in the summer of 2000, though it wasn't straightforward. The ball was set rolling when the contract offer for another year appeared. Less money was on the table, but there was the carrot of a testimonial. Deacon felt the one rather defeated the other, but after no little discussion, a package was agreed, and the testimonial stood. One of the highlights was one of the events that raised one the smallest sums, the £1500 that came out of the race day at Cheltenham barely reflected the enjoyment of the day itself. The year ended with a match against Rotherham at Kingsholm, which Gloucester won, Deacon claiming one of the tries.

Unsurprisingly, given his fifteen years at Gloucester, Deacon has a view about most things, but they're not ones he often shares with wife Karen. While the families of other players are watching from the sidelines, the Deacons are absent. His father goes shopping on a Saturday afternoon, and you won't find his mother in the crowd either, but they have supported him in other ways. Going on tour shortly after Andy and Karen were married was a struggle, so Deacon's father would pay for his place. As for Karen, she's normally at home on a match day, forever looking at her watch.

It may sound awful but I get in a real state. I know how committed he is, and that Andrew will always give 130 per cent. If he was dying he'd probably still go training. If he didn't feel well when he was at Whitbread he'd still go to work. We've been married for sixteen years and when the final was televised against Northampton, I was on the edge of the sofa all the time, and our daughter Emily had to go out. She couldn't stand it. Between 3.00 and 4.45 I'm always thinking about the game, hoping he's OK and hoping they're winning. I might as well be there really I suppose.

The retirement of Darren Garforth at Leicester leaves Deacon as the elder statesman of the Premiership, but it's not a position he wants to give up. His fitness now is of a greater concern to him than ever before, so much so that he did two weeks training on his own before Gloucester's pre-season programme began on 1 July. He's actually heavier now, at more than 17 stones, than he was as an amateur, when he was sometimes criticised for being too light for a prop, but he's more than comfortable with it. He worries too about his performance, aware that he is filling the boots of possibly the best player in the world in his position. Win, lose or draw, after a match Deacon will focus on one poor scrum rather than all the things that went well, and eagerly await the chance to put it right both in training and the next match. He works too hard at his game to enjoy making mistakes, and he retains that edgy attitude that always seems to have existed at Kingsholm down the years.

Throughout my rugby career we've always been up against it. We used to be very insular in our thinking. It was as if the club couldn't see their hand in front of their face. It was almost 'we're Gloucester, we'll be OK'. Everybody hated us. I think it was borne out of England selections – people not going to the right school, getting the right degree, that sort of thing. People say they don't hate us now but I wonder. It's not so long ago that we were fifteen run-of-the-mill blokes who would

A rare treat: Deacon gets his name on the scoresheet against Bath in 1996.

work hard during the week and then become sportsmen on a Saturday. The thing was that we'd get 10,000 people turn up to watch. We'd play elsewhere and there would be so-called stars watched by one man and a dog. They couldn't work it out. I remember a game at Quins once when I sat down next to Will Carling in the press conference afterwards. Everyone was talking to him, and yet we'd won. Only one bloke asked me what I thought. That's the sort of thing that sticks in your memory. We've never got much recognition.

On the basis that it only takes one bad apple to ruin a basket, Andy Deacon is rightly seen as having Gloucester at his core. He's an old-fashioned prop who plays the game in a modern fashion. While the likes of Burton and Blakeway were primarily known for their work in the scrum, Deacon is closer to the style of a Vickery or a Woodman, though he accepts those two are taking prop forward play onto another level again, adding outstanding handling skills to outright strength. Moreover, he still enjoys that unique dressing room banter.

You ask any of the boys and they'll say I'm the most miserable bloke in the world. Some of them bawl and shout, but I'm not like that. I prefer to be quiet, and because I'm older than them as well, they think I'm a miserable *******, but then Gloucester people love to moan. It's the way people are round here. I have to say if we had a chipper at referees like a Martin Johnson or a Lawrence Dallaglio, we'd be a better team, but both Jake and Vicks lead by example. Phil does question things a bit more but only because he's been in that environment where people do. I couldn't be a chipper because I don't have the status, and it's because of that I think Johnson and Dallaglio get away with it. They're almost bigger than the game because the referees have the tools to sort it out, either by moving them back ten yards or issuing a yellow card, but how often do they do it?

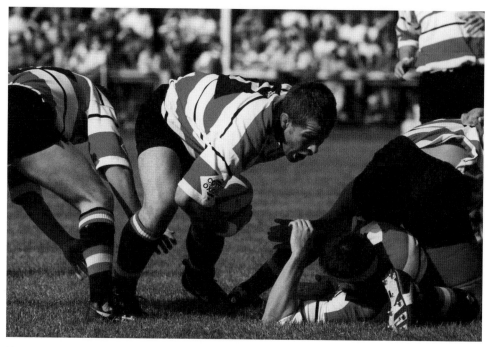

Evergreen: Andy Deacon, driving Gloucester forward for more than a decade.

Deacon's contract which he signed in the summer was his sixth one-year deal as a professional. Prior to that, he'd had two years as one of Gloucester's original intake after the game went open in the summer of 1996. Now as the senior professional, he's more than just a mentor to young players like Marcel Garvey. Apart from words of advice and encouragement, he's also an oracle of information to new signings, and he's stored a few games in his memory that stand out above the rest. The final day clash with Saracens in 1996, the home win over Bath the same season, the victory over Leicester that blew their Championship chances the following year, and the away Cup win over Bath in November 2000 when John Brain prepared and picked the team. It was a week when Philippe Saint-André's absence from the club suggested he felt his side had little chance, only for the players to prove otherwise. Oh, and this year's Cup run, which included a win over Leicester in a match that was vital to them with their poor League form. But what about the future? Deacon will be 39 next July. He'd love to play until he's 40, and he's enjoying every minute mixing it with players from all over the world in his own back yard.

We've been very lucky at Gloucester, in that we've had very few poor foreign players. At the start Terry Fanolua bought into the whole Gloucester thing massively, and Richard Tombs was a huge success. I was good friends with him when he was here. Some of the others, like Stephan Sanchez, didn't get a real chance, but I have no problem with paying a foreign star a million pounds a week so long as he does it. If that's his market value then you pay it. Look at Ian Jones. He was going to retire when he left us, went to Wasps and was player of the year. These guys are very professional. That's why I don't have an issue with the likes of Thinus Delport and Jake Boer. They may play rugby because of the financial benefits but they perform. For me someone like Pucciariello was a disaster. He was on good money but he didn't do anything. My parents drilled it into me to work hard and I've always done that. I think the team have too, but despite us being at the top of the game since it was first played in England, and constantly in the top division since the Leagues were formed, people still used to see us as underdogs. It's quite strange now being favourites to win things.

Andy Deacon was once described in one of those pocket rugby annuals as one of Gloucester's 'powerful and durable props'. He's given up a lot for rugby. As an amateur he sacrificed family life and social activities with the children to get treatment or go training, and he's never commanded the fancy salary of an England international, particularly a back. In return though, he has the respect of all his opponents – respect which he holds as equal to, or even greater than, a solitary cap – and having started his first full season as a professional at the age of 31, he's enjoyed an Indian summer in a career which would be the envy of many. The Shed love him, but for Deacon the famous Gloucester supporters aren't as conscious an influence as you might think.

The thing with our crowd is they are noisy. Other grounds have the same amount of people and they may be passionate, but they're quieter with it. Gloucester fans are a different breed. It's good before the start and you can hear them in a game, but ask me who I'm trying to win the game for and it's for me and my family. I'm selfish like that. I don't mind them having the bargaining rights over other fans because of the result but I'm trying to win for the other fourteen guys out there and because I work bloody hard at what I do. It's nothing to do with anyone else. If England are winning, then more people want to watch club rugby, and that's great. It's like a snowball. In the long run it helps Gloucester, we sell more shirts, and so on and so on, but all I'm really bothered about is Gloucester. Karen's dreading it when I finish playing, but here and now I plan to play for Longlevens. If I look at an all-time list of Gloucester players, and see where I am, I'll probably know a lot of those people. It would be nice to be remembered in the same breath.

I don't think Andy Deacon has any worries on that score.

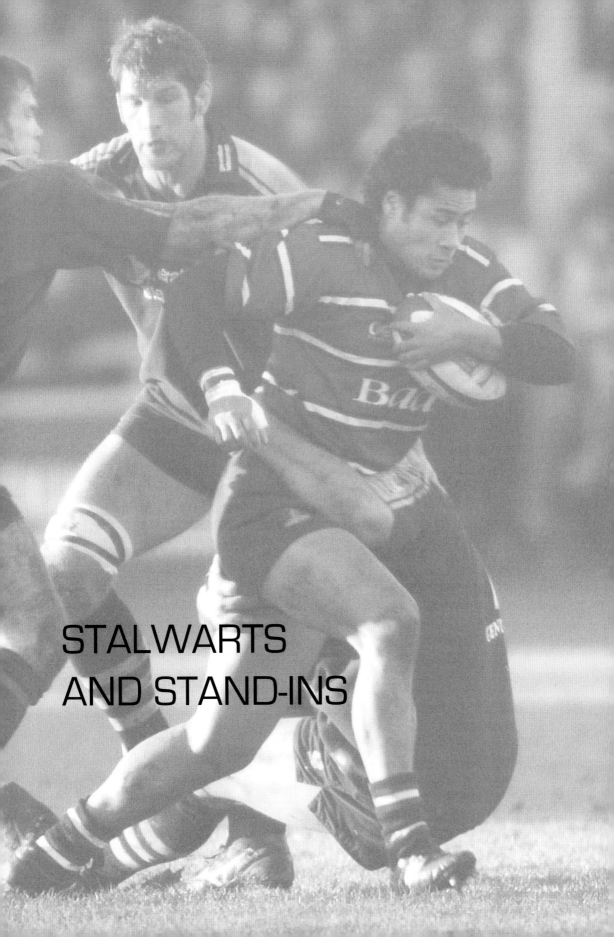

STALWARTS
AND STAND-INS

While moving house two years ago, one of the jobs was to box up my collection of match-day programmes. At the time they weren't filed in any particular order, but having gone through them, I couldn't find one earlier than the modest offering for the fixture with Bridgend on New Year's Day, 1973, Gloucester's centenary year. It cost just 3p, contained a pencil drawing of Gloucester cathedral on the front, and some 'Kingsholm Kackle' from Arthur Russell on the back. Arthur's notes advertised the up and coming County Championship match with Oxfordshire, for which grandstand tickets would be 60p! A far cry from today, but I digress. That programme was actually just one sheet of paper, almost exactly the size of this book, folded in half, so I thought it would be appropriate at this point to create a programme of a similar style, for an imaginary match to be staged on Kingsholm. The question then was how to decide the teams.

For many supporters of a certain age, 'club' matches have either never existed or if they did, they weren't important. You have to go back to the early 1990s to find a mixed schedule of league, cup and friendly matches, but since the Courage League was introduced in 1987, what has evolved into the Premiership has been the domestic benchmark – a standard by which a player's contribution could be reasonably measured. So it is for this game. I'm indebted to Stuart Farmer, the official Zurich statistician, for his work in confirming the appearances for every player who has represented Gloucester in league rugby, which has enabled me to come up with the two sides.

The Stalwarts XV should need little introduction or explanation. In a balanced team, maybe with one compromise which I'm sure you'll spot, this is the most experienced XV Gloucester could have fielded at any one point since the leagues began. A lot of the players cover the period immediately before and after the game became professional, and although they didn't all play at the same time, it doesn't look a bad side. It's interesting to note the lack of foreigners.

With all due respect to them, the Stand-Ins XV should be no match for the Stalwarts. Here are a group of players who singularly failed to make any impact in league terms at Gloucester. They are not the only players whose starting appearances are in single figures, but again the team had to be authentic. Their tally of appearances and points, like the Stalwarts XV, is given alongside each player. I know which one I'd rather see running out of the tunnel.

No doubt many supporters will have views about the best flanker, loose head prop or inside centre they have seen. These two sides haven't been picked on talent, but, I suppose, on their all-round rugby value. Clearly, it is only a snapshot as at the end of the 2002/03 season. In another twelve months, three of the current squad – Gomarsall, Boer and Paramore – may have forced their way into the Stalwart's side. Andy Deacon's contribution has already been acknowledged, but there are five other players who deserve special mention. It seemed only right they should meet in an exclusive club after the match.

THE STALWARTS XV

15   TIM SMITH
        Appearances 94. Points 596

14   PAUL HOLFORD
        Appearances 56. Points 85

13   TERRY FANOLUA
        Appearances 108 + 4 reps. Points 130

12   DON CASKIE
        Appearances 90 + 3 reps. Points 17

11   CHRIS CATLING
        Appearances 104 + 8 reps. Points 128

10   MARK MAPLETOFT
        Appearances 71 + 4 reps. Points 836

9   MARCUS HANNAFORD
        Appearances 64. Points 49

1   TONY WINDO
        Appearances 86 + 3 reps. Points 45

2   CHRIS FORTEY
        Appearances 56 + 47 reps. Points 15

3   ANDY DEACON
        Appearances 124 + 20 reps. Points 40

4   ROB FIDLER
        Appearances 142 + 9 reps. Points 30

5   DAVE SIMS
        Appearances 130 + 8 reps. Points 43

6   PETE GLANVILLE
        Appearances 68 + 6 reps. Points 15

7   IAN SMITH
        Appearances 108. Points 25

8   STEVE OJOMOH
        Appearances 62 + 15 reps. Points 35

THE STAND-INS XV

15 PETER HART
   Appearances 3 + 4 reps. Points 0

14 RAPHAEL SAINT-ANDRÉ
   Appearances 4. Points 0

13 ALASTAIR SAVERIMUTTO
   Appearances 6 + 1 rep. Points 20

12 ALESSANDRO STOICA
   Appearances 4. Points 0

11 DAVE LOUGHEED
   Appearances 2. Points 0

10 PAUL BEECH
   Appearances 7 + 1 rep. Points 28

9 CHARLIE MULRAINE
   Appearances 3 + 1 rep. Points 5

1 STEPHANE SANCHEZ
   Appearances 2 + 8 reps. Points 0

2 HILTON BROWN
   Appearances 1. Points 0

3 DARREN MOLLOY
   Appearances 1 + 1 rep. Points 0

4 COLIN GIBSON
   Appearances 1 + 2 reps. Points 0

5 CRAIG GUEST
   Appearances 1. Points 0

6 KOLI SEWABU
   Appearances 3 + 8 reps. Points 20

7 ROB YORK
   Appearances 1 + 1 rep. Points 0

8 MARK NICHOLLS
   Appearances 4. Points 0

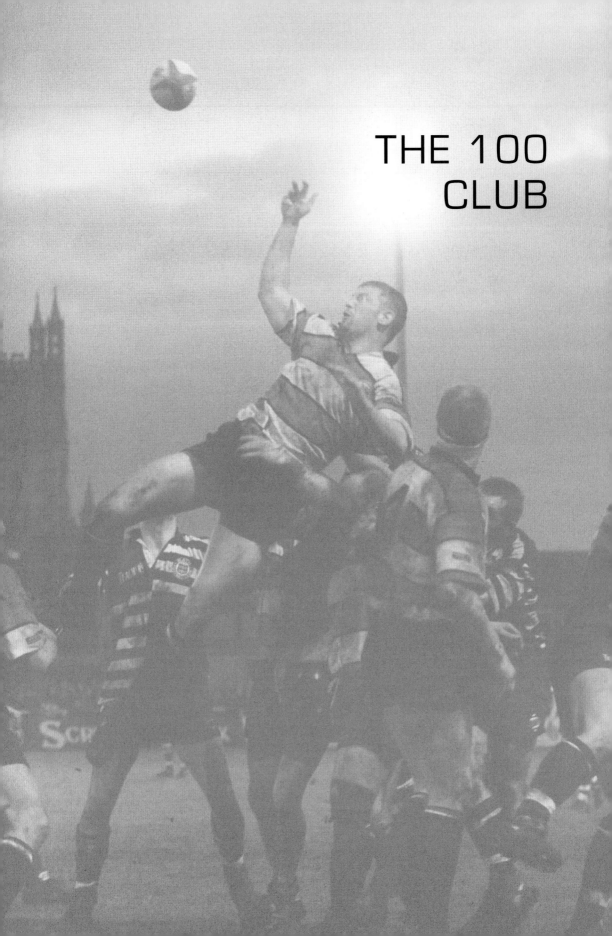

THE 100 CLUB

CLOCKWISE FROM TOP LEFT: Dave Sims, Rob Fidler, Ian Smith (CENTRE), Terry Fanolua, Chris Catling. (www.gpaimages.com)

While Andy Deacon's time at Kingsholm transcends the two domestic Cup finals, the Gloucester side has been dismantled and rebuilt several times over the same period. Loyalty was prevalent in the amateur game, but increasingly now it's a question of players being hard-nosed about contracts that are offered. Five men – Alan Brinn, Bob Clewes, Peter Ford, Richard Mogg and Dick Smith – made over 500 appearances for the Cherry & Whites in their careers, but sixteen years after the league pyramid was formed, it seemed appropriate to mark the contribution of the modern generation – men who have started 100 league matches for Gloucester. Deacon apart, again, there are only five, with just one of them still on the Kingsholm payroll.

CHRIS CATLING
Date of Birth: 17.06.76   League career: 1996-2003
Appearances: 104 + 8 reps Points: 128

Chris Catling joined Gloucester in the summer of 1996. He was studying statistics and operational research at Exeter University, and still had his final year ahead of him. A late developer, he had played several sports to county level at school, but had only broken into representative rugby at the age of 16. While at Exeter he devoted more time to rugby than any other sport, and got as far as the England Students squad, which is where Richard Hill, who was combining work with England A with his job at Kingsholm, first spotted him. Several clubs were chasing him that summer, including Bristol, but with Mark Mapletoft making noises about moving from full back to outside half, there appeared more opportunity to claim the number 15 jersey at Kingsholm. Catling duly signed for Gloucester, and was on the bench for the opening match of the new season at Harlequins. He soon established himself as a first-team regular, although his first year at the club was a testing one.

I remember being quite daunted by it all. It was an English squad, and the club were trying to keep as many Gloucester boys in the pack as possible. It was still a big thing at the time. We only had about ten full-time professionals and the rest of us were semi-professional, which suited me perfectly, but I drove 50,000 miles that year. I used to come up for training on Mondays and Thursdays, and do my own conditioning work in between. Exeter was on the corporate run for graduate recruitment, and a lot of my friends took financial jobs in the city, but I didn't have that decision to make in the final year. I remember there were only six weeks between the end of the season and

Home run: Catling attacking against Perpignan at Kingsholm in the Heineken Cup, 2002. (Bruce Seabrook/www.gpaimages.com)

my finals, so I crammed a lot of work into that period. It was crazy really, but I managed to get a first-class degree. Players who study now have a lot more demands placed on them by their clubs, so they risk missing lectures and not getting work in on time. I think you have to study locally.

Catling's prowess under the high ball and his adventure in running from deep positions soon saw him tagged as 'the best counter-attacking full back in the country'. England A caps followed, but a call to full international level never came. People observed him as a poor kicker, focusing more on this weakness in his game than on similar flaws in other players. There was an element of surprise when he once dropped a goal in a match at Bristol. His strength was more in his positional play, being able to read the game, and assess where to start attacks from. For five seasons under Richard Hill and Philippe Saint-André, he was one of the first names on the teamsheet.

I look back at the Richard Hill era quite fondly as it was my introduction to professional rugby. Things were all very structured. Everyone knew the one thing we would do from any set position on the field, which was quite limiting in a way but we had limited resources. I remember we did about half a dozen sets of bleep tests one season and when one lot didn't come back too well he got rid of Paul Balsom, who was the fitness coach. Richard expected people to put in as much effort as he did, and for me if you see someone putting in the hours I'm more likely to mirror them. There were guys who wouldn't or didn't want to follow that ethos, but Hilly was always on their backs.

Philippe changed things massively. He brought in Bernard Faure, who was a marathon runner, and we'd have sessions where we would just run for an hour. Some of the big guys got really fit but the explosive athletes found it hard. In terms of the backs, coping with running lines and timing, he was probably the best. He'd always jump in and take part, and nine times out of ten he'd get it right, but he didn't have the understanding for the forwards. The language was a problem too. I think that's where he struggled trying to coach lots of players at one time.

Catling joined Gloucester in a closed season when Richard Hill signed sixteen new players. His friendship with Mark Mapletoft has remained long after Gloucester's top point scorer in League rugby left Kingsholm, and locals such as Mark Cornwell and Chris Fortey now count Catling as one of them. It's such spirit which helped the blonde-haired full back through two difficult seasons. In the summer of 2001 Italian Alessandro Stoica was brought to the club by Philippe Saint-André to bolster his options in the back division. Stoica could play at full back or centre, but Catling played in five of the first seven Premiership games until he damaged his shoulder against Bristol. He didn't play again for five months, and had only three more starts at the end of the season. Last season he started only two games – in the Cup against Exeter and in the Premiership away at Leeds. The season ended with Catling being released, and the club needing to find a new PRA representative.

Andrew Stanley had done the players' representative job before me. Damien Hopley from the Union came down one day and I asked a few pertinent questions in the meeting, which perhaps was the wrong thing to do! It was Pete Glanville who suggested I took it on. It is important to have a voice as a group of players, and some of the PRA meetings were really interesting when you saw what they were trying to do. Some people have reservations about it but you only realise what a

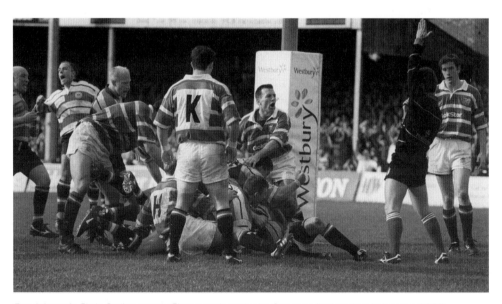

Breakthrough: Chris Catling scores Gloucester's try in the Cup semi-final against Leicester, 1997.

Union is doing and can do when things go wrong, and for the lads at Gloucester that hasn't really happened. I feel I've got a year and a half to make up now. If you're injured you know why you aren't being picked, but otherwise it's horrible. That's why I went on loan to Worcester in the end. The facilities and set up there are excellent, and I felt better in myself just playing again. It didn't look as if the management were going to move Henry Paul from full back, then Munster happened and Thinus Delport was switched there. That's professional sport for you.

Chris Catling is 27. His seven-season stint at Gloucester may have tailed off towards the end, but he remains fit and his keenness to continue as a professional player has taken him to France and the Beziers club. He'll be remembered for once scoring a hat-trick of tries in the Premiership against Newcastle, and for being part of the side that beat Llanelli in the Heineken Cup at Kingsholm thanks to Elton Moncreiff's injury time dropped goal, though he was at the bottom of the ruck at the time, and didn't see it go over. He rates Kingsley Jones as the best motivational captain he played under, and, having spent so long on the sidelines in the last two seasons, he became very familiar with the gym at Kingsholm.

All round the room there are motivational messages. I think the one in front of the squat rack was 'opportunity is seldom realised until it has gone.' Another was 'there is always room for improvement – it's the biggest room in the house'. Everyone takes different ones on board. Overall I had a brilliant time, and I enjoyed living in the area. I only stood in the Shed once, and that was when we beat Leicester 32-30. I'll remember that. My friends who went into the city are just starting to realise the fruits of four or five years of hard work, but I wouldn't change anything. Nigel Melville and Dean Ryan are very shrewd. They always said that if teams started playing like us we have to get up to the next level. I think if the side keeps progressing they could yet be European champions. I just wonder what it'll be like if I get the chance to play at Kingsholm again as an opposition player. Maybe I will.

Maybe.

DAVE SIMS

Date of Birth: 22.11.69   League career: 1990-1999
Appearances: 130 + 8 reps Points: 43

In this exclusive group, there is one full back, one centre, one prop and one flanker. The other two men are both locks, men who Bill McLaren would delightfully have referred to as 'being in the boiler house'. Dave Sims was one of them, and is says a lot about his partnership with Rob Fidler that the pair are virtually neck and neck in terms of League appearances for the Cherry & Whites.

Sims went to Churchdown School – the same one as Mike Teague – and amazingly, is another product of the junior system at Longlevens, which also produced Malcolm Preedy, Neil Matthews and Simon Devereux. Alan Holder and Steve Day take the credit for moulding Sims there, though he might not have been a rugby player at all. He played basketball for West Midlands Schoolboys, and was offered a scholarship to go to America when he left school.

It was Paul Christensen, who still coaches the Gloucester Jets, who got Sims interested in the game, but the raw 16-year-old didn't feel he had enough skill and so declined the opportunity, and you wonder if Dave's rugby career might be seen in a similar light – that of a missed opportunity. Not by me, but by him.

Sims was a 20-year-old rookie when sat on the bench for the 1990 Cup final against Bath. He'd played mostly United rugby that year, but at 25 he had advanced enough in terms of his game and reputation to be named as Gloucester captain for the season after the 1995 World Cup. He was working as a Youth Development Officer at the club when the game went fully professional, having no trade to call on, and some of the old amateur habits were hard to shake off.

I think I should have taken the fitness more seriously and not drunk so much, but that was part of the crack and part of being in the side. Tony Windo and I used to be first to get changed after a game so we could drink as much of the free beer as possible before the old boys came in. In those days the wives and girlfriends came into the club afterwards before we all went into town. By the end it was frowned upon to drink at the club so we'd just arrange to meet later anyway. The young boys – Trevor Woodman, Chris Fortey and Phil Vickery – all liked to party, and if you trained hard all week I couldn't see anything wrong in enjoying yourself on a Saturday night, so long as you went for a run on a Sunday morning. Richard Hill used to say to me 'Simsy, if only you could get fit.' He used to claim I was the most unfit second row in the world. I wasn't but it was just that Pasty (Mark Cornwell) was really fit. He could run like an antelope. Richard knew I'd come from old school rugby, and it would be hard to change me into anything else. I could have changed, but I was a bit too big for my own boots I suppose.

Despite this, Sims' relationship with Richard Hill was very close. He was already captain when Hill arrived, a role he retained the following year, and was given the job for a second stint after Pete Glanville's solitary season as skipper. The pair had first met as players in a South West representative side, where Sims admired Hill's passion for the game, and it was something Sims regarded highly when Hill was brought to Kingsholm in September 1995.

You would talk to Richard and you would get 100 per cent honesty back. He always wanted to win and you knew he wanted to win. He'd scream at you two inches from your face in the dressing room. We had some fantastic results under him and the sprit reminded me of the old days. He was living it with you, and he brought the best out of the players. He also laid down the foundations for Philippe too, building the side that got him success. I thought the way the club treated Richard when he left was disgusting. He'd signed Richard Tombs and Terry Fanolua. Tombs was a decent bloke, never big headed and always good for the team, and Terry may as well have been born in Gloucester. He bought into the whole club thing – except he'd be on the Jack Daniels and Coke when we were on the Strongbow.

Flying high: Sims leaps in the line-out against Bath, April 1996.

Being a first-team regular at Kingsholm had been Sims' main aim in life since he was invited to go on tour to Portugal in 1988. It was to be Keith Richardson who gave him that opportunity initially, and his feelings for the club were shown both in his on the field attitude and, until late in career, his off the field loyalty. In 1992, Wasps came calling with an offer to play for them. Sims was unemployed at the time, and there was a job offer tied in. Sims stayed because chairman Peter Ford put Sims on the payroll at his fruit merchants business, though when pressed on the matter, Sims admitted the work nearly killed him. Ford had been used to getting up early all his life and playing rugby as well, not something that the Sims body clock could cope with. He was grateful, but not half as appreciative as when Brian Glanville, father of team-mate Peter, offered him the chance to work for his tyre firm instead. Dawn starts were confined to the past, and professionalism was the next step, the culmination of a learning curve helped greatly by the players around him.

Captain's duty: Sims signs autographs for a group of fans at Kingsholm.

A lot of players left in 1992, and for me the saddest of the lot was Mike Hamlin. I thought he still had a lot to offer. I remember going to a Chinese restaurant with him after a game once – and he was just talking rugby all the time. He offered so much guidance. Andy Stanley was the same as the United captain. He was one of the most inspirational people I've ever met. He could galvanise any team. I'd like to think they both helped me as a captain. I'd try and find something inspirational to say but I'd leave one or two of the senior players to shout and bawl. I felt a quiet word with people was often better, and in my time I never had a problem with any of my players. They always gave everything, which was all I asked.

Never was that more the case than on 5 April 1997. Sims' wife Jill was in labour at Gloucester Royal Hospital, with Dave at her bedside. Gloucester were at home to Saracens, and when Nathaniel arrived shortly before two o'clock, Sims stayed as long as he could before nearly crashing the car during the short drive to Kingsholm. Saracens had French centre Philippe Sella in their side, and when he got stuck at the bottom of a ruck early on, Sims recalls all the Gloucester players piling in. A memorable day was complete when Mark Mapletoft dropped a goal to clinch a 9-6 win.

Sims is now 33 and has one year left on his contract at Exeter, who play in National Division One. He spent part of the summer doing odd jobs at the ground, including painting the dressing rooms, shades of the old days at Gloucester when he would find any job between the seasons just to keep financially afloat. 'If' can be a big word, but you wonder what might have become of Sims had he taken other routes in his career, and it's a thought that has obviously crossed his mind too.

I never really wanted to go anywhere. I stayed at Gloucester out of loyalty to the people who had brought me through — people like Mike Hamlin, Andy Stanley, Ian Smith — and because the supporters treated me superbly. In hindsight, had I been at another club, I might have been someone who gained big time from being professional, and I might have got thirty England caps rather than three. We were considered as **** by everybody. If I had been sensible I should have swallowed my pride and stayed when they turned me down for a joint testimonial with Tony Windo. I was earning £50,000 a year then. I had a year left on my contract and might have got another one, but the letter from John Fidler about the testimonial destroyed me from the inside. I'd even bought a house on the strength of getting it. I wasn't happy with the way club got rid of Phil Greening, and I became disillusioned, especially when I found out what I was earning in relation to other people. Money was never a big motivating factor for me, but Scott Benton was on £85,000 and the foreigners were on a lot too. I only had one meeting with Philippe Saint-André, who basically said I was to do things his way or leave. I was 29 and needed to be playing, but if you don't have the backing then there's no point in being there. I didn't want to fester.

Sims left Gloucester after eleven seasons and joined Worcester before moving to Devon in the summer of 2002. He now lives there too, but still watches Gloucester's progress with interest, especially that of Trevor Woodman and Phil Vickery, teenage party goers in his team, but, in Sims' judgement, always destined to become superstars on the rugby field. His greatest memories include beating the Irish Presidents XV before the 1991 World Cup, lifting the Cheltenham & Gloucester Trophy against Bedford, and watching chairman Alan Brinn chain smoking in the tunnel of the old wooden stand at Franklins Gardens throughout the Cup semi-final with Northampton in 1990.

It had been his intention to end his playing days by putting something back into the club, playing for the Gloucester United side and helping others, in the way Andy Stanley and his contemporaries had done for him. That wasn't as it turned out, and though there has been life beyond Kingsholm, you sense for Dave Sims, it has never been quite the same.

IAN SMITH

Date of Birth: 16.03.63   League career: 1987-1996
Appearances: 108   Points: 25.

Ian Smith was the first Gloucester player to reach the landmark of 100 League appearances for the club, and he still has an engraved glass decanter to prove it. He is one of three in this select group to have come from Longlevens to Kingsholm, and he's one of two to follow in the footsteps of his father in representing the Cherry & Whites. Dick Smith, also a flanker, stands second in Gloucester's all-time list.

Ian started this season with a new job as director of coaching at Cheltenham, but the majority of his career at Gloucester saw him combine rugby with his job as a civil engineer. He was educated at Sir Thomas Rich's school in the city, and his first job was in the County Council surveyor's department in 1982, the year he went to Kingsholm as a player. The ground, though, had been a regular haunt when he was a boy.

I was aware as a youngster it was a rugby household. We used to go down on a Saturday and watch the old man play. There was a gang of half a dozen of us from the age of seven or eight. I was never pushed into it although I was quite athletic at school, but because of the environment I suppose it got set in my mind that rugby would be the route to take. We were living in Longlevens at the time, so I joined their junior section. A man called Derek Cook ran the team I was in right up until we finished at Under-17s. We'd won the Under-15 Cup, and we won the Under-17 Cup in my last year, when I also played for Gloucester United against Pontypool alongside Viv Wooley and John Watkins. I'd played a bit for the Colts before that.

Smith's consistency of performance and good fortune with injuries meant that the 1990 Pilkington Cup final was his 200th Gloucester appearance, but some significant milestones were still ahead of him. He was to captain the team for three seasons, and, despite being born in Gloucester, he was to become a regular fixture in the Scotland side under coach Ian McGeechan.

My father's parents were from Aberdeen, and we used to spend quite a bit of time with them when I was small. I always supported Scotland in the Five Nations, but playing in England I never thought I would be selected. We'd knocked Nottingham out of the Cup in 1990, and they had a giant lock, Chris Gray, who was in the Scotland set-up. Somehow he'd found out I had some Scottish lineage, and he offered some advice about how I might break in, as I wasn't really aware of a vehicle to do it. About three days later the phone went. This guy said he was Ian McGeechan, and I thought it was a wind up. I gave him all sorts of stick on the phone, only to find out it was him. He said he'd been watching me, there were some 'B' internationals coming up, and he would be keen to see me play. It was embarrassing but encouraging. I eventually made my full debut against England at Murrayfield in 1992.

Smith never scored a try in a Scotland shirt – something he was teased about incessantly – and at Gloucester too he was more concerned about his role in the team, making sure the side clicked as a unit. He had started at Longlevens as a centre, but, on his own admission, he was fed up with not getting the ball, so moved into the back row so he could get it for himself. Clearly the ethos of ten-man rugby extended outwards from Kingsholm in those days into the other city clubs that provided such a nursery of talent, but Smith had built up a bank of knowledge that would be invaluable when the players at Gloucester voted him in as captain in the summer of 1991.

Flanker is a good position to captain a side from. You can see what the tight five are doing in front of you, and what the backs are doing behind you. You get a good feel for the game, which is handy because you are the bloke who is often first to the breakdown and starts the next attack. I always thought I read the game well, in terms of where we should be taking the next phase. I wasn't afraid to chip in with ideas, and then you become mature enough when you think you can do it yourself. Initially I did tend to lean more towards the backs than the forwards, possibly because I wasn't the biggest and wanted to try and be creative. I remember doing extra sessions in the gym with Mike Teague to make me stronger so I could adapt to the grafting side of the game, and from then on there was more of a balance.

The work ethic installed by Derek Cook in those Longlevens days was to stand Ian Smith in good stead for the best part of twenty seasons of rugby, a time span that took him from Colts rugby to a World Cup with Scotland in 1995, where he played in the 89-0 thrashing of the Ivory Coast. He confesses to remembering little about the matches, but the informality of the trip contrasted in stark fashion from the serious mood experienced by club mate Richard West in the England camp.

The inaugural party was in Cape Town. We were based in Pretoria, and we had to travel to Johannesburg by bus to catch the flight to get there. I remember two of the players – Bryan Redpath was one of them – missing the bus and getting left at the hotel. We'd been going about half an hour when a taxi pulled up alongside us on the motorway with these two waving through the window. Remember rugby was on the verge of going professional. We then met up with the England squad, all of them smart in their suits, but none of them were smiling. They hadn't been allowed a drink for two weeks. There was no drinking ban on our trip. It's funny but I watch internationals now and I can't imagine myself ever having been out there. It's like a blur, which is a shame.

Smith returned to Kingsholm to help out Nigel Melville with the forwards immediately after Melville was appointed in March 2002, but his playing days at the club were effectively over earlier than he would have liked after Scotland's summer tour to New Zealand in 1996. Smith played only a handful of games that season before opting to take the path trodden by Mike Teague before him, and join Moseley.

Outnumbered: Ian Smith against London Scottish, February 1992.

Double century: Ian Smith on his 200th appearance against Bath in the Cup final 1990.

I never really wanted to leave Gloucester. If you started rumours that you are unhappy then sometimes offers would come – but I didn't, so there were never any offers. I came back from New Zealand and Richard Hill put me in with the Development squad, which is where the young kids were. It was heartbreaking given the time I had been there and the family link, although that shouldn't have been a reason to pick me. Richard set out his thoughts and I wasn't playing, and other clubs could see that. I remember chatting to Scotland coach Jim Telfer about which offer to take because Bristol, Harlequins and Moseley were all interested. I didn't fancy the travelling to London, so that ruled Quins out, and I had spoken to Moseley about the possibility of going into coaching. I was 33 so time wasn't on my side playing wise. In the end I opted to go there, and was still selected by Scotland even though Moseley weren't in the top division.

Professional rugby never really saw the best of Ian Smith. Tom Walkinshaw's involvement in the club was still several months away when fourteen years service at Kingsholm as a player came to an end, but you sense he enjoyed it as it was. The camaraderie with Derrick Morgan, Marcus Hananford and Pete Jones, all of whom started at Longlevens; the droll humour of John Brain, and the fun often instigated by Jim Breeze and Dave Spencer. Times that are relived in the Cherry Pickers charity games, staged on a handful of occasions each season. The side, which is run by another of Smith's contemporaries, Don Caskie, contains many old favourites – Blakeway, Gadd, Sargent, Teague et al. – and gives them a chance to turn back the clock. Smith likens it to a special club, and despite what happened against Bath, he rates the 1990 side as the best Gloucester team he ever played in.

Sometimes an era of players comes together, and then, no matter who is in charge, it blossoms. I think Nigel and Dean had that last season, and Keith Richardson had it with us. He told us the basics, never ranted or shouted, and we all bought into his ideas. I vividly recall the win at Wasps in the Cup. We had gone there in the League and got hammered (29-4), but we thought if we could invite them into a physical game we could sort them out. They couldn't get their back play going and Richard Mogg won the match with a try in the last couple of minutes, right by the posts. Revenge was sweet.

Gloucester supporters will wish Smith well in his new role, but a word of warning for players and committee alike at the Prince of Wales Stadium. At Gloucester, stories of his generosity abound. He was renowned for never carrying money, partly, he says, because in those days he never had any. It's a tag that's proved difficult to shift over the years, no doubt due in some measure to his Scottish connections. On that basis, the bar tab under his name may do modest business in the months ahead…

ROB FIDLER

Date of Birth: 21.09.74   League career: 1995-2003
Appearances: 142 + 9 reps Points: 30

As it was for Ian Smith, it's a 'like father, like son' story for Rob Fidler. His father, John, was part of the 1978 John Player Cup-winning side, and was a regular in the successful County team of the 1970s. Rob was educated at Cheltenham College, where he first met Tom Beim, who was in the year below him. They were team-mates for two spells at Kingsholm, but were good friends long before that. Now established as a lock, it seems strange to think that as a boy Fidler played initially as a tight-head prop, but it wasn't long before a growth spurt took him out of the front row. He dabbled a bit as a no. 8, but didn't settle, and went on to captain the College's first XV from the second row. County and England Under-19 honours indicated his potential, and he'd just completed the foundation year of a sports science degree at Loughborough University when a full-time contract offer arrived from Gloucester. Rob didn't need asking twice.

The year I was at Loughborough I played mostly United rugby, but I did sit on the bench for the first-team occasionally. People ask me if I was lucky to be turning professional at 21. I'm sure I would have played as an amateur if everyone else had been an amateur. The IRB probably decided to make rugby professional because otherwise there would have been so many deals and back handers going on the game would have become very corrupt. It was a case of having to open it up. I was just stumbling into my proper degree course at the time – so I suppose I was fortunate.

Fidler's attributes at Gloucester were his application to the honest and often unsung work of a lock forward in tight areas, and winning his fair share of ball as a front jumper in the line-out. His partner on many occasions was Dave Sims, another member of this exclusive group. Rugby partnerships tend to be thought of in terms of the backs – half

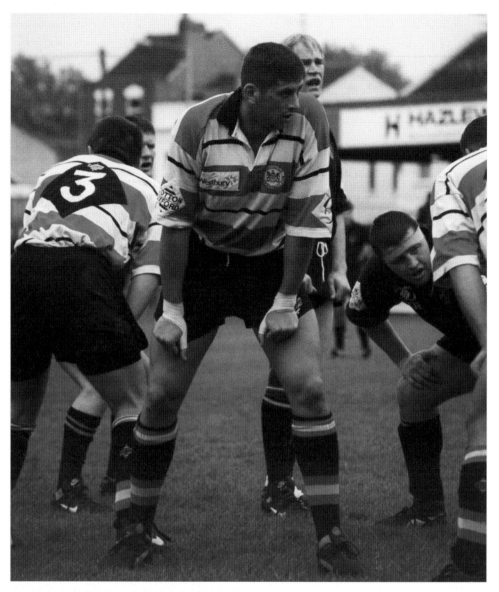

Front jumper: Rob Fidler waits against Bath at The Rec.

backs and centres in particular – but here was a lock partnership that seemed to work too. It's unusual to find one player who has every skill, and here were two who had different strengths and complemented each other as a result. Fidler was the younger and less demonstrative half of the duo, acknowledging that Sims was a man who led by example and was an inspirational figure to the rest of the team. It proved to be Richard Hill's first-choice pairing, yet ironically, when Sims was out of favour at the end of the 1998/99 season, it was Fidler who captained the side in the cup semi-final at Wasps – only, apparently, because no one else volunteered. By that stage Hill had left, but Fidler is one of a clutch of former players to hold him in high regard.

Richard gave us a real shake. He knew what he wanted and was very dedicated, and I bought into that really because I was just coming into the side and didn't know anything else. Some of the older boys were a bit set in their ways, and were just enjoying being paid to play. To me he brought a lot of good qualities from Bath, where he'd been in a successful team. He tried to convert amateurs into professionals, and instil the winning attitude that he'd experienced at the Rec. He was clever when he went looking for players because he always wanted them to be ones who would fit into the Gloucester mentality. Bearing in mind we'd had no sort of success for quite a while, I thought he did a good job.

Now 29, you might think that Rob's international career is probably behind him. His two caps were against New Zealand and South Africa in 1998, on the same trip that Dave Sims won his three. At that stage, Hill was still in charge at Kingsholm, and his style was mirrored by forwards coach John Brain, who would get Rob and the rest of the pack to practise rigorously so that everyone was clear about their roles. You wonder whether if Gloucester had been more successful, Fidler's international career might have been longer, but he's not bitter about any missed chances.

We had to start with hard work and determination and go from there. It's now got to the stage where Dean Ryan is doing the fine tuning with the forwards. He's trying to create a way of playing that other sides can't cope with. There are more tactics talked now than ever before, but each of the coaches could only work with what they had. Each took it as far as they could, and then someone else has moved it on to the next level. It has been like three stepping stones in my career, with Richard, Philippe, and now Dean and Nigel. If you look at the international squads we've always had a good sprinkling of players on the fringes. There were

Like father, like son: Rob with father, John. Both won full England caps while playing for Gloucester.

always a good crop of Gloucester players in the England A side (Fidler played at that level fourteen times) but that didn't translate into full caps. Even this year when we've done well it's been the same, but playing for your country is a goal you set and I can say I have an England cap.

Fidler's Gloucester memories are varied. Watching – and I use the term loosely – a game against Auckland as a boy in thick fog, where Gloucester lost 34-3; being badly run around at both Sale (52-12) and Bath (71-21) in 1997, just as the Tom Walkinshaw era was starting; the friendships among the diverse personalities in the dressing room; the winning of those benchmark home games against Bath, Saracens and Leicester, and this year's Powergen Final; and the game at Thomond Park against Munster, which, in many ways, was *the* story of last season.

From a playing point of view to concede that last try was a massive disappointment, although Munster were a very clever team that day. They knew what they wanted to do. I think we tried to stop them doing what they wanted to do, rather than doing what we wanted to do, and there is a difference. The tackle count was almost double what it would be in an average game. We'd played well against them at home, and we had a side that if we'd performed we could have secured a place in the next round – but it was just one of those days that happen in sport.

Fidler's new challenge is to try and help Bath through a transitional phase. His contract was up last summer and after initially being told he was in Gloucester's plans, he became concerned at what was going on around him.

People were getting signed up, but I was told they would get to me in due course. Then I was told the priority was to sign players in positions where the club needed them, and they wouldn't be able to sort anything out for me until after that – which may mean not at all. The Premiership season was over by this stage and clubs were busy signing players and finalising their budgets so I had to get something sorted out. I let my agent know and Bath said they were still looking for a second row. There were a couple of other enquiries but thinking about it now it was all done very quickly.

Not many players over the years have gone from Gloucester to Bath. Several in the modern era have come the other way – McCarthy, Ojomoh, Pearce and Sanders are the best examples – but Fidler should be assured of a warm welcome on his return. The Gloucester fans, like those of all the top-flight teams, have come to realise that players don't often play their entire career at one club any more. He'll be in familiar surroundings though. When training at Gloucester, he always used the away dressing room, with his peg opposite Andy Deacon. The temptation on a match day, if his concentration isn't total, might just be to turn left and go into the one marked 'home'. Maybe he'll just pop his head round the door…

TERRY FANOLUA
Date of Birth: 3.07.74   League career 1997-2003
Appearances: 108 + 4 reps   Points 130

Terry Fanolua started the season as Gloucester's top try scorer in League rugby. His tally of twenty-five is level with that of the departed Chris Catling, and six more than both Tom Beim and Mark Mapletoft, who are next on the list, but that statistic is just one small element in the Samoan's contribution at Kingsholm. Fanolua is now in his seventh season at Gloucester, having signed in the summer of 1997. One of eight children, he was working as a courier driver when the opportunity came to travel halfway round the world and play rugby professionally. It wasn't a chance to be passed up.

I was only 22 and had no commitments. I had started playing rugby at about 6 years old, and used to watch games every Saturday afternoon in Samoa because my older brothers, cousins and uncles all played. There was a big celebration when our village, Lotosoa, won the Shield, which is the main competition in Samoa. At school and in club junior teams I was a fly half. It was only when I moved into senior club rugby I started playing at centre.

It's a position Fanolua has made his own at Gloucester, although he has filled in at full back, on the wing and at fly half on occasions. As he adjusted to the huge difference in culture after he agreed to join the club, Fanolua's first year saw him bugged by homesickness. He couldn't settle and although he still misses his family and looks forward

Try: Fanolua scores against Sale, April 2003. (www.gpaimages.com)

to those precious trips back to Samoa, in Gloucester his partner Ann and his daughter Tara now play a big part of his life. Inside the club too, time has seen him mature from a quiet character into one who takes his full part in the dressing room banter, and few enjoy playing the game more than the man the fans call 'Tezza'.

I love every minute of it, and I've learned something from everyone. When Richard Tombs and I arrived no-one had heard of us, which was probably why we did well in our first season. Then we became tightly marked and it was like running into brick walls all the time. As for the coaches, Richard Hill was very much an 'in your face' character, and Philippe was unorthodox but very passionate. Nigel is calm and structured. He makes sure everyone knows how we are going to play and how we are going to defend and I think that's why we had success last season.

Fanolua's popularity with the Gloucester supporters comes from his no-nonsense approach. If Jake Boer is the John Gadd of his time, Fanolua is the John Bayliss – defensively solid and someone you know will take the ball through the midfield with real guts. He played through the climax to last season with a hernia that needed a summer operation, and you sense there are always niggles that might keep others on the sidelines – although that's merely a by-product of the way he plays.

Our culture back home is to enjoy the physical side of the game. To me tries are a bonus. If one comes then I'll take it but I'd rather give the last pass than score myself. You mustn't be selfish and I think that's one of my strengths. My concentration used to be a weakness but it is better now and I read the game better too, and to me making a big tackle to stop a try is actually more satisfying than scoring one.

While worries persist over the top English players becoming burned out with the increasingly hectic calendar at all levels, to Fanolua it's not a new concept. After a fortnight's rehabilitation following his hernia operation, he went on a six-match tour with Samoa which included a Test against Namibia. He had only one week's holiday before flying back to Gloucester, by which time the start of the Premiership was less than a month away. Fanolua accepts that sooner or later his body will give up on such a punishing schedule, but if his mental ambition is anything to go by it'll be mind over matter for some time yet.

If people aren't ambitious they shouldn't be at the club. When I first arrived we were happy if we could just win all our home games. Now we're expected to win home or away, and winning the cup final against Northampton was unbelievable. I had never played in front of a crowd like that before. I'm always nervous before a match but I try not to show it and during the final I felt the body language of the guys said we weren't going to lose, even though it was a tiring game. We put the squeeze on after James (Forrester) scored and everybody put their bodies on the line. It was awesome.

Fanolua is in the last season of his current Gloucester contract, and while he won't admit to targeting any one particular competition, you sense he'd love the club to have some success on the European stage, especially after being part of the Munster mauling last

Tenacious: Fanolua in action against Wasps at Kingsholm, January 2003. (www.gpaimages.com)

season. With 108 appearances from a possible 136 league matches, the 29-year-old Samoan has been a major player in Gloucester's transition from makeweights to heavyweights in the Premiership. Moreover, he's been firmly adopted as one of their own by the Gloucester rugby family – much to the amazement of his parents.

When my Mum and Dad came over to watch they couldn't believe people were chanting for me, and that supporters were wearing shirts with my name on the back. They were absolutely thrilled, and it made me feel I had done something good for my family. I was proud too – but I also feel privileged to be part of this great club.

The elite nature of this group can be shown by the fact that no-one can join them this season, and only Mark Cornwell has a realistic chance of doing so by the summer of 2005. It is mathematically possible that Jake Boer could reach this notable landmark in the professional era by the same stage, but he would be required to start thirty-nine of Gloucester's forty-four Premiership matches – a tall order. It would be fair to say that the club has shown loyalty to all the players concerned, but the reverse is also true, and with several big names leaving England for French clubs after the World Cup, it is loyalty that is becoming increasingly rare in the cut-throat drive for success. Fanolua, of course, made his Gloucester debut in September 1997 – on a day when the impact of Tom Walkinshaw's arrival as chairman was seen on the field for the first time by the supporters.

THE GALLIC
SHRUG

CLASSIC MATCH 5

20 May 2000, The Stoop Memorial Ground, Allied Dunbar Premiership
London Irish 40   Gloucester 42

Gloucester's season reached an astonishing crescendo at the Stoop as they clinched third place in the Premiership with their sixth away victory. It was a match that had just about everything, and the leaping delight shown by skipper Kingsley Jones was mirrored around the Gloucester bench when prop Adey Powels, who had never previously scored in the Premiership, touched down for his second try of the match in the last minute. Powels and Andy Deacon both spent ten minutes in the sin bin in separate incidents, which made Gloucester's win even more remarkable.

Both teams made a mockery of any idea this would be a gentle end of season affair. Jarrod Cunningham kicked an early penalty for the Exiles after a full scale fracas between the forwards and five tries before the interval set the tone for what was to follow.

Gloucester, ragged one moment and exhilarating the next, produced a breathtaking move that Irish could only halt by giving away a penalty. Adey Powels tapped the ball to himself and dived over for his first-ever Premiership score. It was to be the only time Gloucester were ahead until he scored again. The Irish response was swift, a powerful drive being finished off by Mike Worsley, and by half-time they had a twelve-point cushion. Stephen Bachop created a try on an overlap for Michael Horak, and then Justin Bishop raced away to score after good work by Putt and Cunningham, who landed two of the three conversions, and a second penalty. Gloucester kept themselves in it with a neat try finished by a stumbling Catling after he was tap tackled, but the build up credit went to Moncrieff, Eustace and Pearce. Mannix converted and kicked one penalty.

The second half was equally eventful. 25-13 down, Gloucester drew themselves level with some inspiring play by Terry Fanolua and Ian Jones. First the Samoan acted as a decoy runner as Mannix and Yates sent Rob Jewell through to score, and then a splendid run by Jones through the middle set up a fine attacking position. Kingsley Jones took the ball on and drew in the cover, and some slick hands made the space for Catling to score his second try. Mannix kicked one conversion before being replaced by Byron Hayward.

Mistakes were plentiful but the pace was unrelenting. Another burst of points for Irish through two tries for wing Hoadley and another for Justin Bishop put them fifteen points up, but fortunately Cunningham was having a mixed day and none of them were converted. Gloucester sensed an outside chance when Adam Eustace sold a dummy to the home defence and cut the deficit. Replacement Mark Cornwell, who only came on with eight minutes left, made an instant impact, dropping on a kick ahead from Joe Ewens after Hoadley and Fanolua both failed to gather, and with one conversion from Hayward Gloucester were within a score. It was left to Powels, the former gas fitter from Berry Hill, to be in the right place at the right time as Gloucester recovered a kick ahead from Ian Jones and spread the ball wide for the matches' twelfth and final try.

The global nature of rugby union after the 'big bang' in the aftermath of the 1995 World Cup took two years to reach Kingsholm. A further two years down the line, and the man who was the most capped international to represent his country while playing for Gloucester had been put in charge of the team. Philippe Saint-André was a first in a number of areas, and someone who in years to come will be talked about as one of the most colourful characters in the club's history.

His contribution as director of rugby at Kingsholm makes it easy to gloss over his time as a player. In two seasons, thirty-one Premiership appearances yielded fourteen tries, yet he found some defences easier to breach than others, having failed to score against Harlequins, Leicester, Northampton, Saracens and Wasps. His brace on his debut against Bristol showed an alert brain and a tactical awareness that meant despite playing outside his homeland, Philippe won the last four of his sixty-nine French caps at Gloucester. With more than thirty of those as captain, he had proved his value was far more than just being one of the most outstanding and intuitive finishers of his generation.

If his acquisition as a player was something of a coup, Saint-André's elevation to coaching the Cherry & Whites was a calculated gamble. Owner Tom Walkinshaw was balancing the probable loss of one valuable cutting edge on the field for a sharper all-round team under Saint-André's guidance, and it didn't take the Frenchman long to see that combining playing and coaching was virtually impossible. He started only three games after Richard Hill left, his last appearance coming in the Tetley Cup semi-final defeat at Wasps. By the summer of 1999, his name, like that of Mike Teague before him, was making players think seriously about coming to Kingsholm, and Saint-André was busy recruiting. Ken Nottage's predecessor, Hamish Brown, admitted a fresh spark was essential.

We had anticipated that English clubs would be back in Europe in the autumn of 1999, and we set a budget to try and make sure we were one of them. It meant putting up admission prices considerably the year before, and unfortunately we didn't get the wins we wanted, which made people more selective about the games they came to. I don't think there were any clubs in the black at the time, we were discussing salary caps, and also looking at working with fewer but better players.

Saint-André's three closed seasons as director of rugby each produced one major acquisition, and the first indication he meant business came with the arrival of Ian Jones. The All Black lock was highly regarded throughout the world, having won more than 70 caps. He was retiring after the 1999 World Cup, but Saint-André was convinced

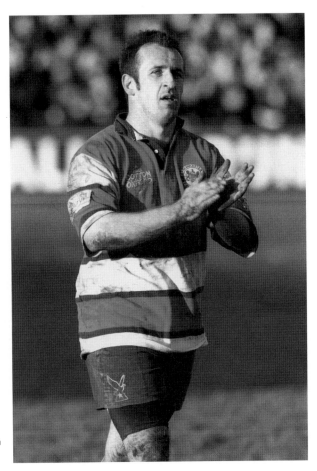

Crossing the boundary: Philippe
playing in the Cup quarter-final
against Harlequins, his first big match
as coach. (www.gpaimages.com)

spending eighteen months at Kingsholm wasn't just a case of Jones creating a pension fund for his family.

I had played with him in the Barbarians team in 1994. He was a winner, a good second jumper in the line-out and keen to come and have success with us. We needed to find a balance. We had some young players, and it was important to have experience too. He was 32, which is old for a wing or a centre, but not for a lock.

Junior Paramore also joined Gloucester that summer, Saint-André snapping up the Samoan from Bedford, who had lost backer Frank Warren, and linking him up with his cousin Terry Fanolua in his Gloucester squad, but those weren't the only changes. It is inevitable that every coach has different ideas, and Saint-André saw plenty of areas that needed work.

When I came to Gloucester my first impression was that although the club was professional, the organisation was archaic. The guys would eat sandwiches and drink Coca Cola between training sessions. I made us all eat together – pasta, chicken – and the drinks were better too. The quality

All Black to Cherry & White: New Zealand lock Ian Jones in the dressing room at Kingsholm with kit-man Mike Potter. (www.gpaimages.com)

of the training improved because I had two very good fitness coaches (Ed Archer and Peter Finch) but it was hard to change the minds of the players. At the start of the season I went round all the pubs to find out if the guys were serious or not but I think they understood.

Saint's Andre's ethos of having a good structure around him was in stark contrast to Richard Hill, who ran things at Kingsholm very much on his own. Philippe's style was to delegate the specialist work, and manage the structure instead, and although probably two thirds of the squad were players he inherited, he takes the credit for taking Gloucester from the lower reaches of the table to the point where they were genuine championship challengers twelve months later. They had lost just once in eleven Premiership matches when they were beaten by Northampton at Kinghsolm in March 2000, a day when Phil Vickery was sent off. Saint-André saw it as a benchmark of Gloucester's development.

We had been tenth the previous year and to try to be in the top five was a big step. Northampton were better than us and every time they had an opportunity to score, they did. We needed five opportunities to score one try, and the quality and skill wasn't good enough.

Kingsley Jones, in his first year as captain, couldn't believe the season had gone so well.

In my eyes it was unreal. I thought the two best teams were Bath and Northampton, and both had been together a lot longer than us. When you build a new team, you add a player here and a player there over time and you end up with a quality side. It was too good to be true really because we won nine on the trot. We were written off because we had a lot of new players so to be fourth at that stage was outstanding for us.

What Saint-André was doing was catching people's attention. Phil Vickery could see the ambition and signed a new contract; Clive Woodward recommended that Andy Gomarsall look at Gloucester when he decided he wanted to leave relegated Bedford; Jake Boer and Robert Todd found the concept of Heineken Cup rugby at Kingsholm more attractive than staying at London Irish. Only John Fidler felt he had to leave. Philippe's off-the-field troubleshooter couldn't run his construction company as well, and so a thirty-year association with the club ended with Fidler hoping people thought he'd done his bit.

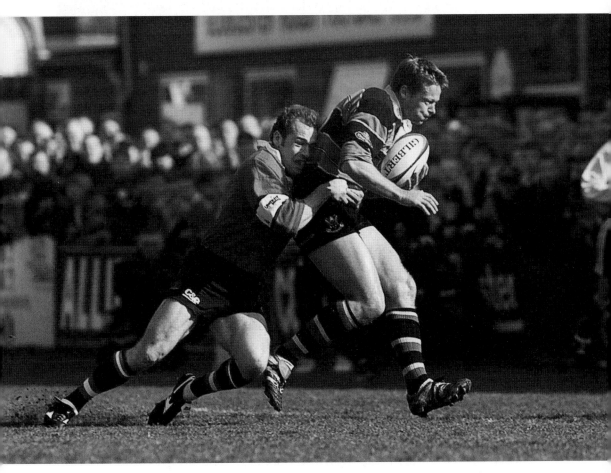

Hanging on: Brian Johnson struggles to tackle Northampton's Nick Beal. (www.gpaimages.com)

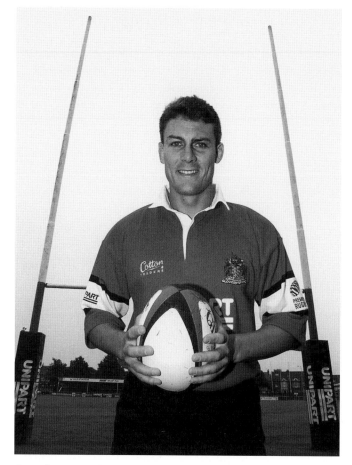

Australian centre Jason Little. (www.gpaimages.com)

We had been through the mill and I just tried to give Philippe all the support I could. The previous year had been particularly hard but the proof was in the pudding. Someone really needed to be at the club all the time, and I couldn't do that. It had been an ambition of mine to put the club back on the map, where we were years ago. It was great being in Europe because it's such a hot bed of rugby here. I just hoped we'd go from strength to strength.

A last day win at London Irish – notable for two tries from prop Adey Powels – appeared to fully vindicate Tom Walkinshaw's decision to give Saint-André his new role at Kingsholm. There had been a significant improvement in the Premiership with a third placed finish, which was enough to satisfy both in the short term, but the development wasn't over. There was still a gap to be bridged in terms of competing with the top English sides, and Gloucester didn't want to be left floundering in Europe. It was time to go shopping again, and back into the southern hemisphere for Australian Jason Little. His tally of caps was up alongside Ian Jones' for New Zealand, and Little admitted a former Gloucester favourite had a hand in him signing for the Cherry & Whites.

I spoke to Richard Tombs, who dispelled any doubts I might have had. He gave Gloucester a rave review and said how much he loved it here. Michael Lynagh also told me that he didn't enjoy playing at Kingsholm for Saracens, so it was good to know that backing was with you rather than against you.

Saint-André was clearly delighted to get his man, and he wasn't put off by Little having had a knee operation just before coming to England.

He proved he was a world-class player having won the World Cup with Australia. He could play inside centre and outside centre, and if my two fly halves are injured he can play there too.

Perhaps that was Little's problem. His twelve months at Kingsholm never really saw him have a settled run in the team in one position, and he'd started only two games before he was fulfilling that key role at outside half after Simon Mannix broke his hand. His departure to Bristol the following summer left you feeling Gloucester hadn't seen the best of him.

By this time eight different nationalities were represented at Kingsholm and there was healthy competition for places, particularly in the back row, where Andrew Hazell was pushing Kingsley Jones hard for the number 7 jersey. Saint-André decided he couldn't have a captain who wasn't sure of his place, so turned instead to Ian Jones. Within six games, four of which were lost, he changed his mind. 'Jones the taller', as the Shed came to know him, had been given too much responsibility. He would be relieved of the captaincy and the forward coaching duties he had taken on alongside John Brain, who was still combining a part time role at Kingsholm with his job at the Trading Standards Office, and return to playing alone. It saw Jones soon return to his best form, but the disruption set the tone for what was to follow. Premiership results, unlike the previous campaign, never showed any positive pattern. Good and poor performances came in equal measure; heavy defeats at Saracens and Wasps, yet solid home wins over Bristol and London Irish. John Brain, who had master minded a Tetley Cup win over Bath at the Rec while Philippe was out of the country, felt the home defeat by Northampton was typical of Gloucester's problems.

We had plenty of chances and missed four kicks at goal, and you can't afford to do that. At times we were trying to play too much and we were making mistakes. We had to look hard at how we could control a game and still lose, because we were getting territory and then not converting possession into points. It was very disappointing.

Things came to a head on 10 February 2001. Gloucester was soundly beaten by Wasps at Kingsholm (28-3) and after the match Saint-André offered to resign – an offer Tom Walkinshaw rejected. Gloucester, for all their progress in Europe, had lost six out of seven Premiership games. It was a run the Frenchman found hard to explain.

It was the worst performance in my two years. I was sick and sad for the supporters because it was not acceptable to play that type of rugby. We made so many basic mistakes. It was incredible that

Right-hand man: forwards coach John Brain.

we beat Cardiff two weeks before and played some great rugby but against Wasps we switched off in the second half. We should have kept the game simple and we didn't, and I think the team had more problems in their minds than with their skills.

It was time to go hunting for new talent again. With only a partial rally at the end of the season – Gloucester finished seventh – disappointment in the Heineken semi-finals and the new Zurich play offs, Saint-André waved goodbye to the half-back pairing of Mannix and Moncrieff, centre Chris Yates, and skipper Kingsley Jones, who had become increasingly prone to injury. Several others on the fringes left too, and Ian Jones asked himself if he could commit for another year at the age of 34. The answer was no.

It was a tough decision. I love the game but I've got a young family. Rugby has never been a job to me. I still have a passion for it and I loved my time at Gloucester. Being involved in the semi-final of the Heineken Cup was a tremendous occasion, but looking forward consistency of management and selection is the key to success.

Jones, of course, re-appeared later the following season with Wasps, having been persuaded to return to playing by none other than Nigel Melville. John Brain stood down as coach of the forwards, only to be unveiled as the new director of rugby at Worcester, and Saint-André recruited Laurent Seigne from Brive to bolster his back room staff. We awaited the customary big name summer acquisition. A little known fly half called Ludovic Mercier arrived from Aurillac, and the options in the three quarters were (temporarily, as it turned out) strengthened by the Italian international Alessandro Stoica. Ultimately, he couldn't handle being without the sun, the beach and the spaghetti. Rumours were rife until 25 July 2001, when Gloucester called a press conference not at Kingsholm, but at a hotel in London. The top table consisted of Tom Walkinshaw, Philippe Saint-André, and rugby league star Henry Paul. After an unsuccessful loan spell at Bath under Brian Ashton, the Bradford Bulls star was coming to Gloucester on a four-year contract.

I was sad to leave Bradford, but then I was sad to leave Wigan before that. I see myself as a role model in the community. My job is to win first and foremost. I train every day because my job is one of the best in the world and I don't take it for granted. Bringing in new players adds a new flavour and excitement. I'd won everything in rugby league and I wanted a new challenge, and I knew Gloucester didn't muck about. You need to play with a passion when you wear the jersey.

It must be said that Saint-André never publicly complained about not being able to sign a player. There always appeared to be the scope to do so, despite the £1.8 million salary cap, and the final decision of who would blend in with the players at his disposal was also his, despite the team he assembled around him. One of the characteristics of his time as director of rugby was the large range of people he worked with. Going through three forwards coaches as well as two for the backs indicates either instability or a constant striving for improvement, depending on your point of view. Saint-André often spoke of the strange way in which he and John Brain, outwardly so different, complimented each other in their philosophy on rugby. The same was true in his relationship with Kingsley Jones, but these were broad strokes on the canvas. The fine detail however, according to lock forward Rob Fidler, wasn't always so clear.

Not satisfied: director of rugby Philippe Saint-André. (www.gpaimages.com)

New boy: Henry Paul is unveiled as a Gloucester player. (www.gpaimages.com)

Philippe was good in that he could spot players but communication was a problem for him. He had ideas in his head but the issue was getting those ideas across. Laurent Seigne was the same. He didn't have the mastery of the English language so that you knew accurately where you were going and how you were going to get there. It was a bit of guesswork on both sides.

What turned out to be Saint-André's final season started with him having to look for a new backs coach just as the Premiership was about to kick off. Andy Keast, who had come to Gloucester for the last handful of games at the end of the previous season, and then signed a two-year contract, left in the week before the first Premiership match at home to Northampton. Keast said he had been marginalised, and that his role as a coach had diminished. Saint-André managed on his own until the former Welsh fly half and Sale director of rugby Paul Turner arrived in October, but his input proved useful as Gloucester enjoyed an improved domestic season.

Henry Paul's integration into the team began at inside centre, and having been tried elsewhere, it now looks as if that's where he is settled. Ludovic Mercier proved to be one of the most accurate and prodigious kickers of a rugby ball to wear a Gloucester jersey, and James Simpson-Daniel, with just half a dozen games behind him at the start of the season, stepped up his development and showed immediately that he was a talent to be noticed.

Saint-André's habit of calling Kingsholm a fortress was borne out by eight wins from their first nine home Premiership games, but away victories were still few and far between – indeed Turner saw Gloucester lose at Newcastle, Bath and twice at London Irish (once was in the Powergen Cup) before the win at Harlequins in what proved to be Saint-André's last match, with the last try scored by Gloucester under him fittingly finished by one of Saint-André's French signings, Olivier Azam.

Philippe Saint-André was the first man to take Gloucester into the Heineken Cup, and he left when the club was well placed to qualify for a second time. He was also the club's first overseas player in the professional era, and will be seen as a key figure in Gloucester's development from a partisan but staunchly local club into a cosmopolitan competitor at home and abroad. He had a feel for the game which took him to the highest level as a player, and possessed an engaging humour which often drew parallels with food. He once famously likened developing a team to making a good mayonnaise. I'm sure nobody outside (or even inside) the club would claim to understand everything he did, but few would doubt he left Gloucester with a stronger squad than the one he inherited. In that sense, he had done a good job, and Gloucester would certainly have been the poorer without him.

Moving on: Philippe Saint-André bids an emotional goodbye to the Gloucester fans at The Stoop. (Bruce Seabrook/www.gpaimages.com)

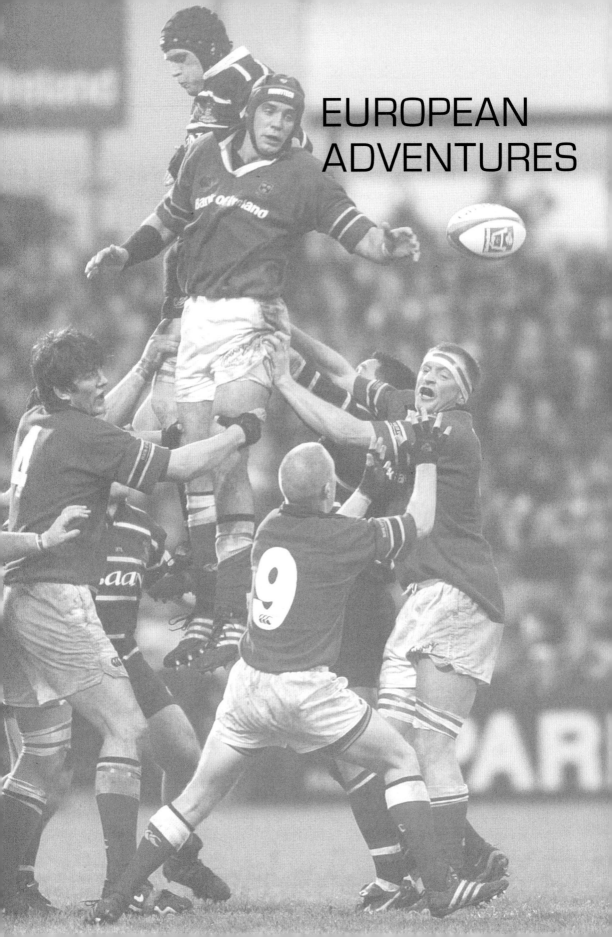

EUROPEAN
ADVENTURES

CLASSIC MATCH 6

18 January 2003, Thomond Park, Limerick, Heineken Cup (pool stages)
Munster 33   Gloucester 6

Thomond Park elevated itself to a state of almost supernatural intensity to inspire Munster to the greatest comeback in the history of the Heineken Cup. Required to score four tries and win by a margin of 27 points, Munster achieved their target in the last minute of normal time. It was a perfectly paced execution, while Gloucester looked utterly disorganised. This was a huge disaster on a big stage.

Munster were methodical throughout. They had a game plan to expose Henry Paul's vulnerability at full back, and the forwards created a platform from which fly-half Ronan O'Gara ran the game with considerable authority. It forced Gloucester to defend for virtually the entire match. They were roughed up in the scrums and line-out, where O'Callaghan was dominant, and Munster carried the ball with considerable power. In the close contact areas they were supreme as well, and the unnerving truth was that Gloucester did not function with any clarity of thought and to a man under-performed considerably. They seemed unable to alter their game plan as the pressure mounted, and the confusion was summed up over a second half penalty. Mercier ran it, where a successful kick at goal could have sent Gloucester through on point difference.

Munster's tries were evenly spaced throughout the match. The tackling of Boer, Buxton, Fidler and Roncero in particular kept them at bay until the 18th minute, by which time Mercier and O'Gara had each kicked a penalty. Then the impressive Stringer nipped away possession from the back of a scrum and wing Kelly surged up the narrow side to score. O'Gara missed the conversion but he and Mercier exchanged further penalties late in the first half. 11-6 hardly looked a disaster until, on the stroke of half-time, Gloucester's defence couldn't cope with a kick slid through by centre Jason Holland. Wing Mossie Lawler dropped on it, and although O'Gara again failed to convert, Munster were halfway to their target.

With the atmosphere rising, Munster's tempo went with it. Their forwards dominated at the start of the second half. O'Gara kicked a third penalty and Gloucester lost Azam to the sin bin. Munster took full advantage. Holland, socks round his ankles, started the late onslaught. Behind his pack on the Gloucester 22, he punted across field into acres of space for lock O'Driscoll to gather on the bounce and score. O'Gara's conversion was an unerring effort, and the thought of Gloucester stealing some points had all but gone. They had to rely on their ability to keep Munster out. They couldn't do it. O'Driscoll won a Munster line-out, and a drive was set up. Staunton tried to bury his way over the line but was held up, and the ball was recycled. Space opened up for scrum-half Stringer, who found Holland and ultimately Kelly on his outside, the wing diving over for his second try of the match. You could have heard a pin drop as 14,000 fans fell silent for O'Gara's critical conversion. He obliged, and Thomond Park exploded for a second time. As Brendan Fanning wrote in the *Irish Independent* on the Sunday morning 'anyone writing a script like this would have been placed in a straightjacket and carted away.' Absolutely.

The 2003 World Cup means that the group stages of this season's Heineken Cup campaign are played between the beginning of December 2003 and the end of January 2004. It is Gloucester's third season in the top club competition in the northern hemisphere, and a competition which the club's managing director Ken Nottage has admitted on more than one occasion his budget cannot do without. They may not have always been successful, but Gloucester have had European games at Kingsholm for six of the last seven seasons – the odd one out being 1998/99 – and perhaps inevitably, there has been a rise in interest since the club qualified for the Heineken Cup for the first time.

The competition was one of the consequences of the game turning professional and, together with the second string European Conference and Parker Pen Shield, it has given Gloucester supporters the chance to watch their side play in Italy, France, Ireland and Spain. They've yet to face a Scottish side, and Welsh fixtures merely rekindle memories of the club's traditional fixture list in the old amateur days.

Gloucester's indifferent league form put them in the European Conference in the first two seasons (1996/97 and 1997/98). Elimination came at the group stage in the first season, but in the second, only an away defeat in France by Toulon (16-13) prevented them going through the pool with a 100 per cent record. It meant qualification for the quarter-finals, but an away draw which sent Gloucester to Paris to play Stade Français, a

Pre-match atmosphere at Stade Français.

Gloucester look deflated after conceding a seventh try.

side who have since developed a formidable reputation. The trip saw BBC Radio Gloucestershire's first overseas commentary at a ground in the shadow of the new Stade de France, with many supporters travelling by overnight coach both ways. If ever there was a trip that galvanised interest in Gloucester in Europe, then that was it. Around 500 fans made one of the stands a vision of Kingsholm, but the continuous band and musical celebrations that greeted every Stade Français try – and there were eight of them – told you that you weren't in England. The match was also memorable for Pete Jones' first game for three years at prop, so given the side Gloucester were able to field, the 55-22 score didn't surprise Richard Hill.

They had bought a good pack of forwards, and we knew they would take us on up front. We gifted three soft tries to them and they slipped through tackles in deep positions for two others. We conceded a try right on half-time to make it 22-10 and although there was some encouraging handling between forwards and backs we didn't defend well enough. Our front-line tackling and organisation had been poor against Saracens and Harlequins just beforehand and once again we leaked too many tries.

The match was to be Richard Hill's last in Europe with Gloucester. The club weren't involved the following year and by the time the 1999/2000 Conference matches got underway, Philippe Saint-André had replaced him as director of rugby. This was World Cup year, Gloucester had been largely unaffected by international calls, and the team had made a bright start with six wins from their first eight Premiership games. Spain were the minnows in the group, Bridgend provided a Welsh flavour, but the key games looked to be the first and the last, home and away against Biarritz. The home game saw a debut try for New Zealand legend Ian Jones, and all appeared well until a sloppy performance at Bridgend changed the shape of the group. The match was drawn 29-29, and the picture was clear. Gloucester would have to win in Biarritz to get through. Once again, as at Stade Français two years earlier, Gloucester would go to France for what was effectively a knock-out game without a goal kicker after Simon Mannix was injured against Spain at Kingsholm. It was a night where Philippe Bernat-Salles, scorer of a famous try in the 1999 World Cup semi-final against New Zealand, ran rings round the Gloucester defence. The game was all but over by half-time, and Saint-André was aware that domestically, the task now was to be in the top competition, the Heineken Cup, the following year.

Biarritz were good in the first half but we were terrible. We missed a lot of tackles and the organisation and concentration were poor. I tried a lot of solutions, changed a lot of players and it was interesting, but the team that won the Conference didn't go into the Heineken Cup. That's why for me I was disappointed but the league was the priority.

It was a setback the team took in their stride before moving on. Six more Premiership wins were enough to secure a place in the 2000/01 Heineken Cup. Bath's win in the 1998 final had set the standard for others to follow, and Gloucester's steering committee were to be an interesting mix – a French legend, a traditional Gloucester lock from the amateur days, and a Welsh flanker who bore the scars from a decade of fierce competition, but who kept coming back for more. It was a vibrant cocktail.

The draw appeared to favour Gloucester. Again they were paired with Italian opposition, with the added benefit of playing the last pool game against Roma in Italy. Surely that was a banker to finish with. Llanelli and French side Colomiers looked useful sides but with two teams possibly going through, Gloucester looked well placed to qualify for the quarter-finals. This they did, but only after putting their supporters through a mangle of emotions.

All appeared well at the start. New Australian centre Jason Little marked his Heineken Cup debut with a try at Stradey Park, and even though Gloucester lost Simon Mannix with a hand injury, an away win at Llanelli set down a marker. The first battle of the war had been won, with Gloucester skippered by their Welsh talisman, flanker Kingsley Jones.

We didn't want to go there and make the numbers up. I reminded the boys we'd worked all the previous season to get into that position and it would be stupid to waste it. We panicked a little when we lost Simon and our discipline fell apart a bit but Jason proved he was a game breaker by scoring a try out of nothing. We had lacked confidence in our defence in the build-up, which meant people were chasing everybody else's tackle if somebody missed one, but on the night we were great.

With two home games to come Gloucester now had it in their own hands to take charge of the group. Tom Beim destroyed Roma on his own with some virtuoso finishing, scoring five of the teams' six tries in the second half, but the script was then torn up by Colomiers. In a Saturday night game at Kingsholm, they stole a try early in the second half and threatened to be going home with a victory until a late penalty try salvaged

Captain Fantastic: Kingsley Jones.
(www.gpaimages.com)

Gloucester a 22-22 draw. It wasn't ideal but it could have been worse, and it left the Cherry & Whites needing to get something from their trip to the Stade Selery to restore their authority. All appeared well for an hour on a gloriously sunny day. Defences were on top, and Mannix and Marticorena were trading penalties. Then, a rare break down the left saw Tom Beim put Chris Catling in the clear to run in behind the posts. Mannix added the conversion and Gloucester had a ten point lead at 19-9. What followed was Colomiers saying 'welcome to the Heineken Cup.' They scored twenty points, including two tries, in the last ten minutes, leaving Mannix, who is no longer playing professional rugby, to reflect on Gloucester being blown away.

A ten-point lead was a good buffer but it was hard to control the territory. I think we put the ball straight out from a restart and we hardly saw it after that, and when we did it was in the wrong areas. We couldn't shut the game down and kept giving penalties away. The wind was swirling and it was very warm but the guys tackled and tackled. We didn't actually play that badly. The dressing room was very quiet afterwards. We knew we could still get through, but that we needed two wins to do it.

It was more than two months later that the pool was completed, and in between Gloucester had come agonisingly close to ending Leicester's unbeaten home record in the Premiership. On that day Freddie Tuilagi had scored an injury-time try, but fate often balances up such injustices, as Gloucester were to find out. The home game against Llanelli was now, effectively, a one off. Assuming they were to beat Roma away, Gloucester could virtually secure their place in the quarter-finals by beating the Scarlets, but if Llanelli were to win, Gloucester supporters could put aside any thoughts of further progress. Form at the time was distinctly average, and prop Trevor Woodman remembers the basics weren't up to the normal standard.

We had been losing the ball in contact and there had been too many errors. We only seemed able to play for one or two phases rather than the eight or nine you need to score tries. We were dropping the ball and giving away easy points through too many penalties. It was my first game in the Heineken Cup, and my biggest Gloucester match – almost like a cup final.

Rarely can a match of such importance have had such a crazy and dramatic climax. If Elton Moncrieff never plays another game of rugby in his life, his name will forever be etched into Gloucester folklore. Llanelli wing Mark Jones had laid down the gauntlet with an early try, and it was left to Mannix's boot to keep Gloucester in the game once Jones scored a second try after half-time. It wasn't vintage fare, but it was edge of the seat rugby throughout. Attacking the Deans Way end, Gloucester were pressing as 80 minutes approached, 27-25 in arrears. You can imagine the thoughts going through the minds of supporters and management alike. League form suggested qualification for the 2001/02 Heineken Cup was unlikely, so this could be the end of a major source of income for two seasons. The chance of a financially rewarding or culturally fascinating quarter-final could be gone too. Yet another Gloucester attack floundered almost under the Llanelli posts, which made what happened next all the more remarkable. Australian scrum half Elton Moncrieff, who frequently looked as happy as a bulldog chewing a wasp, retrieved the ball from the ruck and went for an outrageous dropped goal. There appeared no way in which he had sufficient room to get the necessary elevation, but the ball struck the shoulder of Llanelli's Daffyd Jones on the way up, and somehow looped over the bar. Cue bedlam in the Shed, in fact, it was bedlam everywhere, and even more so when the injury time had elapsed with no further score. Llanelli, beaten by a Paul Grayson penalty for Northampton in the semi-finals the season before, had been dealt a cruel hand once again, and Moncrieff accepts the result may not have been fair.

I don't know if we deserved to win. We were a bit lucky with my kick being deflected, but we accepted it. We had kicked the ball away too much and made too many errors, and so were fortunate to come up trumps in the end.

Financially, it was a huge result for Gloucester owner Tom Walkinshaw. With just three home Premiership games after the end of January, another full house for a home quarter-final would be a huge bonus, and he too accepted the ball had bounced Gloucester's way.

It was a good game between two physical, evenly matched teams. There was nothing in it, just the rub of the green at the end. We've just got to keep plugging away. We're still developing and you're going to have some ups and downs along the way until we are proficient at playing this new style of rugby.

Gloucester left Kingsholm that night grateful for the draw they had been handed. Roma, the weakest team in the group, stood between them and the quarter-finals – the only question if they won was whether they could sneak a home draw as one of the top four qualifiers. The match in Italy threatened to be a rout early on, as Gloucester raced into a 25-3 lead midway through the first half, Mannix again kicking superbly, but a sloppy period just before half-time set the tone for a nervous second forty minutes. Only a late try from Jason Little enabled Gloucester to breathe easily in the closing moments, but forwards coach John Brain recalls looking at the line-up in the last eight with a degree of satisfaction.

It wasn't necessarily the biggest day in the history of the club but it was an important milestone. Winning the group was a goal we had set ourselves. We were in the quarter-finals, and sides like Northampton, Wasps, Saracens and Bath hadn't made it. We then had to wait for Cardiff's game in Toulouse, because we knew if they were beaten, we would probably play them at home in the quarter-finals.

Drop of fortune: Elton Moncrieff watches his kick against Llanelli. (www.gpaimages.com)

Just two weeks after the drama against Llanelli, Kingsholm was again a cauldron. Cardiff had surprisingly lost in Toulouse, and in so doing relinquished the considerable advantage of playing at the old Arms Park. For Gloucester, it was another benchmark of their progress in the twenty-two months since Philippe Saint-André had been put in charge, and the Cherry & Whites director of rugby was happy to play up the Welsh club's credentials.

I spoke with the coach of Toulouse and the Cardiff team don't have a lot of weaknesses. They have one or two world-class players. I tried to sign Neil Jenkins before the 1999 World Cup but the WRU said if he signed then they wouldn't pick him. I am a young coach and for me and the club it is a big match, and I think the supporters must be proud of the team. People are surprised by my selections, but sometimes when we play away, not everyone is keen to play. All the team wants to play in this game, and I think the pressure is on Cardiff.

It was pressure that proved too much. Gloucester captain Kingsley Jones had sensed a cocky attitude when Cardiff arrived, and felt it might be Gloucester's day. The discipline was good, and the penalty count low. Gloucester squeezed Cardiff out of the game for forty minutes, but went to sleep at the start of the second half and conceded a try before their grip on the game was regained.

They may not have scored a try, but a 21–15 victory put Gloucester into the semi-final draw. Moncrieff's dropped goal looked to have turned the season, and Gloucester were drawing on all the experience of Jason Little and Ian Jones to steer them through, but they didn't fancy travelling to Ireland to play Munster, or France to play the much improved Stade Français in the semi-finals. The draw spared them either trip, but instead paired Gloucester with a devil they knew – Leicester.

By this stage Andy Keast had joined Gloucester as backs coach on a temporary basis, and there was the bonus of Phil Vickery being fit enough to return to the front row after a muscular injury. The match, peculiarly played at Watford despite noises about going to either Stoke City's new Britannia Stadium or the Madjeski Stadium at Reading, was one where Kingsley Jones felt Gloucester had no room for error.

When you play Leicester you worry about them in all departments. They can mix their game up, but I thought we had a pack which could cause them trouble. Our problem was that when we were competing in both the Premiership and the Heineken Cup, it was hard psychologically to keep focused all the time. We could beat Cardiff at home and lose badly away at Harlequins. On our day we could be as good as anyone defensively, so I thought the game might be decided by a mistake or a breakaway. We certainly couldn't afford to let Leicester get ten points up.

In fact, they never were, but neither did they lose. Gloucester scored first through a Mannix penalty but weakened by injuries that saw Byron Hayward at full back and two double barrelled rookies on the wings (Rory Greenslade-Jones and James Simpson-Daniel) they were chasing the game from the moment Tigers centre Leon Lloyd ran in under the posts midway through the first half. The only try of the match was a controversial one, as Phil Vickery remembers.

The French referee (Joel Dume) made the decision and no amount of moaning by us would change it, but having thought it was our advantage, he then thought a kick to them, and then them running it back to us was still an advantage to us. I didn't understand it, but Leicester knew how to win and that shone through. Even when they were on the rack they were competitive and had confidence in the people around them. We tried hard but there was a team that was confident and there was a team that was half confident, and that's why we had an indifferent season.

Clearly there is only a small margin of improvement possible if Gloucester are to better that inaugural Heineken Cup campaign. Perhaps it may come this season, although the draw, pairing them with Bourgoin, Munster and Treviso, has hardly been kind. Munster have had a role to play before, as we shall see, but Gloucester, as Kingsley Jones intimated earlier, had thus far found it hard to concentrate on more than one competition. A good league season had coincided with poor form in Europe and vice versa. Consequently, they were back in the second string competition, now called the Parker Pen Shield, in the autumn of 2001.

The group stages of this competition proved a mismatch for an improving Gloucester side. New talent was coming through in the form of Forrester and Goodridge, and there was a new inside centre too – rugby league legend Henry Paul taking his bow against Caerphilly. It didn't prove too taxing as Gloucester racked up a record 98 points a week after starting the group with a win over La Rochelle. Paul scored a try and kicked ten conversions just ten days after arriving at Kingsholm.

Thank you:
Phil Vickery
acknowledges the fans
after the defeat by
Leicester.
(www.gpaimages.com)

The gulf in standard between some of the sides involved was amply illustrated again later in the group stages, Darren O'Leary helping himself to five tries as Gran Parma conceded 99 points without reply. A win away in France against La Rochelle, despite Trevor Woodman being sent off, meant Gloucester cruised into the quarter-finals with a 100 per cent record. A home game against Ebbw Vale shouldn't have posed too many problems, but hampered by dreadful conditions, and the loss of Adam Eustace with a broken leg, Gloucester only got going in the second half, where four tries clinched what in the end was a comfortable win.

By the time the semi-final came round in early April, Gloucester had a new man at the helm, their third director of rugby in the professional era. Nigel Melville had arrived from Wasps in what was almost a no-win situation. With Gloucester well placed in the league, and in the Parker Pen semi-final, people would expect Heineken Cup qualification and, accepting that knockout rugby can throw up some surprises, some silverware either from the Shield or the end of season play-offs. It was a zero or hero scenario, and just as Elton Moncrieff's dropped goal was the most unlikely end to the Heineken clash with Llanelli fifteen months earlier, the Shield semi-final with Sale was also decided by a last gasp kick.

This time it was Gloucester's French fly-half Ludovic Mercier who was in the spotlight. The Cherry & Whites had raced into an early 13-0 lead before Sale scored 28 points without reply either side of half-time. Gloucester rallied, but still trailed when they were awarded a penalty just 15 metres out in the last minute. Mercier, normally so secure, missed, and Sale sneaked into the final by a single point. It would have been easy to blame Mercier but Melville looked at the bigger picture.

Tense moment: Ludovic Mercier
sets himself for the decisive kick
against Sale.
(www.gpaimages.com)

We kicked the ball a bit too long, they off loaded well and when you are playing that sort of rugby with pace it is hard to contain. People make plans for Jason Robinson but you mustn't forget about Cueto and Hanley. Teams always come back at you in semi-finals because there is so much on them. You'd have put your mortgage on Ludo getting that kick but Sale kept the ball well and we let in a couple of tries either side of half-time which were important.

In terms of incident, Gloucester's European adventures have given full value for money since that match in Paris against Stade Français. The cliff-hanging finale against Llanelli; the bravery against Leicester; the record-breaking scores against Gran Parma and Caerphilly, and the agony against Sale. Did I say agony? Little will compare on that score to events on 18 January 2003, which, if measured on the Richter scale, would have been one of the most significant earthquakes in Gloucester's history, parallel perhaps with the defeat by Bath at Twickenham back in 1990.

Once again, the Heineken Cup ignited the imagination. For the first time, Gloucester were drawn with an Irish team in their group. Munster were a provincial side with huge experience, twice beaten finalists, but thought by some pundits to be past their best and in need of rebuilding. The French flavour was provided by the catalan side Perpignan, while Viadana, from Italy, weren't expected to do anything other than gain further experience. They, at least, followed the script.

Gloucester's clashes with Munster were at either end of the sequence, starting at Kingsholm and finishing at Thomond Park, where Munster had never lost a Heineken

Cup match. Nigel Melville, now with Dean Ryan at his side, had got Gloucester firing on all cylinders in the Premiership, and Ryan felt it was an advantage to start at home against one of the favourites.

You have to respect what they have done on the European stage. They are a very patient team and while the ball might not be fizzing about, their game doesn't lack intensity – you want to try and be in there knocking them over. The Kingsholm factor was always going to be a concern for them, and we were playing well in the Premiership, scoring a lot of points in second halves after doing a lot of damage in the first halves. It was up to us to maintain what we'd been doing in a different environment.

It was a task Gloucester managed superbly, once again grinding down the opposition before forcing the pace in the second half. 35-16 and four tries to one told its own story, but the group was far from over. As expected, Viadana were brushed aside, Gloucester managing a dozen tries in an 80-28 romp in Italy, before Perpignan looked uncomfortable on a bitingly cold day at Kingsholm. Young wing Marcel Garvey scored two second-half tries, and Gloucester had three straight wins behind them. The hardest part of the group was still ahead though, and given that Gloucester had won only twice from six previous attempts on French soil in Europe, hooker Olivier Azam urged caution.

I knew some of the Perpignan players from the French team and also from playing against them. Leicester played them the previous season and had real problems with them, and they were low in confidence at the time because they weren't doing well in the French league. I knew we had to be careful.

The match proved that there were genuinely three teams who had hopes of making the knockout stages from Gloucester's group. Fly-half Manny Edmonds controlled the match, the Cherry & Whites never got a foothold in the game at all, and two late tries by Boer and Mercier gave the result a flatteringly close look at 31-23. I remember standing in the airport alongside Phil Vickery for the return trip. He had a high-quality black eye and stitches in the eyebrow above it. Perpignan had ridden roughshod over Gloucester and Nigel Melville knew it.

They had power and used it. They got more phased ball going than we did and had more measured control at half back. We gave a cheap try away just before half-time which was our own fault, and by then we were seventeen points down. Our ball was slow. They were better than we were and deserved to win on the balance of play.

Gloucester now knew the equation. Barring a miracle they would now need to win in Munster to guarantee the home draw they craved in the quarter-finals, something no side had previously done, and no one knew how hard that would be better than Melville. He'd played there with Wasps (and lost, of course), as well as twice taking his former club there on pre-season tours. He knew it wasn't posh, and that it had a spirit about it. It was something he would have to tackle once Gloucester had seen off Viadana at Kingsholm. This Gloucester finally did, but it took the introduction of James Simpson-Daniel as a second-half replacement to kick them into overdrive. Fit again after a bout of glandular fever, Simpson-Daniel scored a try and inspired a late flurry of points in a 64-16 win on a day when the pitch was covered until the last possible moment after a week of hard frosts. The Munster rematch would decide Gloucester's fate. A comic strip couldn't have made up anything more dramatic.

The last weekend of the pool stages saw Perpignan going to Viadana as likely second qualifiers in the group. Assuming they won, Perpignan would finish with eight points. Gloucester already had eight and Munster six, so Gloucester could draw at Thomond Park and still finish top. Munster had no option but to try and win as well as they could, and hope. Gloucester looked to be in pole position but Phil Vickery, now in his second season as captain, felt it was all or nothing for both teams.

Munster are a fantastic team. I'm sure they'll throw something at us the like of which the boys have never experienced before because there's so much at stake. If you've got Williams, Stringer and O'Gara at 8, 9 and 10 you're going to control games. They've won before when people haven't given them a hope and they'll be smarting having lost at Kingsholm, and that's where we want to be in the quarter-final. We can't go out there trying to draw or trying to lose by a few points, we have to go out there and try to win.

Gloucester's first-team coach, Dean Ryan. (www.gpaimages.com)

Munster magic: Alan Quinlan leaps in a line-out at Thomond Park. (www.gpaimages.com)

Walking around Limerick on the Sunday morning after the match, there was a sense of having witnessed a truly great sporting occasion. Like many who travelled from Gloucester, I had arrived on the Friday to see this rather spartan venue, with three sides open to the elements. The transformation was as great as that of the Munster team, who were so tepid at Kingsholm. Fuelled by the most passionate crowd at a club ground I can remember, Munster scored four tries and won by a margin of 27 points. It was precisely what they needed to do to send Gloucester from first to third in the group, and leave Perpignan, no doubt much to their surprise, as pool winners after their win over Viadana.

The question then was why did it happen? All the talk before the match had been about wanting to win, yet somehow within the dressing room that drive to win was lost. Gloucester appeared content to contain, and when Munster went for the jugular, Gloucester couldn't respond. Dean Ryan confesses he was concerned after Mossie Lawler's try late in the first half.

The Irish supporters celebrate with a pitch invasion at the end. (www. gpaimages.com)

We felt at half-time we were in a bit of a negative frame of mind, and that cost us in the end. We didn't get the ball in key areas, and when we did we lost it and lost the field position. O'Gara kicked superbly and he protected the Munster 22 to an extent where we couldn't get in there. We offered brave and committed defence but under constant pressure for 80 minutes we were going to creak somewhere, and it hurt.

Veteran prop Andy Deacon was one of the shell-shocked team to leave the pitch in disbelief.

Munster had pace in their game all the way through, and as for the crowd, I've never heard anything like it in my career. We had put pressure on ourselves because of how we had done, and the players in the sin bin didn't help. We'd had some highs, but that was a low.

Financially, it was a huge blow for managing director Ken Nottage.

We had budgeted to reach the quarter-final. In terms of cash flow that result cut off a source of income that could have contained a semi-final or even a final. It put extra emphasis on making the Zurich play off final at the end of the season and making progress in the Powergen Cup.

Gloucester's recovery from the Munster debacle made the events of that weekend even more remarkable. Only at Leeds were they to taste defeat in the regulation Premiership season, and their consistency answered any questions about the resolve of the players. As luck would have it, Gloucester once again have to compete with Munster for a place in the quarter-finals of this seasons' Heineken Cup. Both could go through of course, but then there's the third element, which involves a double header for the Cherry & Whites against their former director of rugby Philippe Saint-André, who is now in charge at Bourgoin. In this particular pack, Gloucester will hope he isn't the joker.

HOLM AND AWAY

When people come from away they can't believe the atmosphere, and I'm so grateful to our forefathers for buying the ground for us in the first place. It's quite something to think that more than a hundred years ago they purchased it, looked after it for a period and then passed it on to someone else. I think if each us who are involved leaves it in a better state then when we took it over I think we've done our job.

Long-serving player and former chairman, Peter Ford, speaking in 1991 on the 100th anniversary of rugby being played on Kingsholm. The first home of the club may have been at the Spa, but its spiritual base has always been on the seven-acre plot bought from the Castle Grim Estate. There has probably been proportionately more discussion about the ground in recent years than at any other time in Gloucester's history, almost certainly because of the rapid pace at which every facet of the game has developed.

Yet until now, things have changed slowly at Kingsholm. Standing on the ground today, Peter Ford would look out on a scene almost identical to the one he saw in the year after that cup final defeat by Bath. Indeed, since the author was first a spectator in 1973, alterations have been minimal, although I am old enough to remember the days when the dressing rooms weren't within the main stand. Former prop Mike Burton does too.

When I started we used to come out from the Shed side and down the steps just where the roof stops. I can remember going into the old dressing rooms and seeing the jerseys hanging on the pegs, and your first home game for the first team is a big game for any Gloucester player.

Thirty years on, there has only been development on one side, with the addition of the hospitality boxes at the Deans Way end, formerly known as 'The Tump'. The Worcester Street end, and 'The Shed' in its current form both pre-date the erection of floodlights at the ground in 1967 with a match against the Bosuns, an invitation side similar to the Barbarians. Gloucester won 34-8. The current main stand was built in just nine weeks in 1933 after the old one was destroyed by fire. After being at the head of affairs for so long, Gloucester have some catching up to do.

Some clubs, clearly ill-equipped in terms of facilities for the professional era and without the capital or room to develop, decided to relocate. Wasps and Saracens have now settled at Adams Park, Wycombe and Vicarage Road, Watford, two established football grounds some distance from their traditional bases. London Irish, the surviving club out of the merger between Richmond, London Scottish and themselves, have left Sunbury for the Madjeski Stadium at Reading. Sale Sharks are the latest to admit defeat, deciding that Heywood Road can no longer cope and playing for the first time this season at Stockport

Centenary scene: a snowy Kingsholm in 1991. Gloucester first played there in 1891.

County's Edgeley Park. As the demands on clubs for certain basic levels of facilities rise, this group have nothing to worry about, although their homes are not their own. Gloucester's planning must show a greater balance between the team and the ground.

Talk of developing the main stand side of Kingsholm, other than cosmetically, has been ongoing for most of the period covered by this book with so far nothing to show for it. Plans were drawn up during Mike Coley's era as chief executive, but outside events were moving so quickly the project was shelved. Architects were involved again in 2000, by which time Tom Walkinshaw had joined entrepreneurs like Andrew Brownsword, Keith Barwell and Sir John Hall in backing rugby's rising status. He could see only one way in which the club would move.

If the spectator base outgrows the stadium we will have to think about relocating, but there's no question of moving the club from Kingsholm providing the capacity is sufficient for the people who want to watch.

It's amazing to think that at that time Gloucester were only averaging crowds of 6,500 for Premiership matches, but there was underlying momentum. The core fan base was growing, the big games were sell outs and within a year Walkinshaw was expressing concerns about Kingsholm's viability.

If we had a ground that could hold between 12,000 and 14,000 we could get crowds like that. I don't know if the site is big enough but whatever we do has to be a complete club decision. At the moment we're struggling with crowds of over about 9,000 because although the ground has a licence to hold more, people can't see. We've got to make sure people want to come and can see the game in comfort.

Full capacity: An 11,000 crowd at Kingsholm causes problems.

All the time the net was being tightened, as Rotherham found out. Clubs had to provide a minimum of 2,000 seats, and the Union were withholding a precentage of their payments to clubs to ensure teams didn't spend it on players and that grounds were neglected. Gloucester's bill for maintenance and annual safety related matters was in excess of £100,000 and it was becoming increasingly obvious that new facilities were needed. Speculation grew about leaving Kingsholm, due to the complexity and disruption of trying to redevelop on the existing site. The Cattle Market and The King's School cricket ground at Archdeacon Meadow emerged as favourtites, but the emotional attachment to Kingsholm kept coming up in the discussions. Now the balance does seem to have shifted, and managing director Ken Nottage says the most likely option is a piecemeal redevelopment of the current site.

Deciding whether we should remodel Kingsholm or move somewhere else is a simple question with a complicated answer. All the work we have done has been simultaneous, but it has been slow. In many ways developing Kingsholm isn't really the right solution. The ideal would be to build a 15,000 capacity facility with the ability to go to 20,000 with more parking, but all the sites we looked at – Archdeacon Meadow, Brockworth, Staverton – either had their own problems or weren't available. At least here modifications are easier to get through the planning stage, and we believe we can achieve a meaningful solution. At the moment we have only 1,248 seats and that is not what you would expect from a premier sporting facility, but we want to maintain terracing on all four sides. I believe the atmosphere comes from the combination of seating and standing, and we have demonstrated that terracing works.

That argument was never more amply illustrated than last season, when for the first time in the professional era, and only the second time in the history of the club, the Gloucester supporters inspired their team to finish the season with a 100 per cent record on their own ground in first-team fixtures – sixteen games against teams from across Europe without a single blemish. For the record, the other season concerned was 1981/82, when under the captaincy of Steve Mills, twenty-eight teams tried to win at Kingsholm without success. It seems appropriate therefore, before considering what the new appearance of the ground may be, to consider why it is such a comfort blanket to the team.

Mark Mapletoft, Gloucester's top points scorer in league rugby. More than 500 of his 836 points came at Kingsholm. (www.gpaimages.com)

Plush it certainly isn't. The pitch is old and doesn't have the benefit of the scientific investment used when installing the playing surfaces at new venues – Andy Deacon, for example, says the best pitch to play on in the Premiership is at the Madjeski Stadium, Reading – but former full-back Chris Catling says it's that earthy nature that makes a big contribution.

I would say it's a package. The pitch can be like a mud bath in January and I'm sure clubs talk about getting a barracking when they come down here, and as soon as you plant that seed, young players in particular must be terrified as to what the full force of the Shed is like.

Dave Sims skippered Gloucester for three seasons, although his memories of the atmosphere go back to his schooldays.

I was taken by my dad to watch the 1984/85 cup semi-final against Bath. Tim Smith had a nightmare but the atmosphere was awesome. It was total intimidation. I was terrified to lose at home. The crowds were bigger at Leicester but they seem further away. I've been lucky in that I've been back twice and had a good reception.

Clearly Sims was one of the Shed's favourites, but down the years they've have their favourite enemies too, and they haven't always been in the opposition. Centre Don Caskie played at Kingsholm for eight seasons between 1989 and 1997.

I can remember Mike Hamlin getting an awful lot of stick, and I used to think if I could hear it, he must be able to hear it as well. I think the fans like this reputation of being very black and white, and liking a hard, no-nonsense type of player, and the reason the club has enjoyed some success is that they have kept people from the start of the professional era – Deacon and Fanolua were there, along with both Woodman and Vickery. That's a core of well-liked players, people the fans can identify with. As soon as the players become untouchable, then you lose everything Gloucester is and was. You can't underestimate what Kingsholm is like, both when you come out to warm up, and when you come out for real. It's a blood and thunder place. I've played for London Scottish against Gloucester and when you're on the Shed side there's nothing like it.

It's not surprising that given this raucous backing, Gloucester's record at home in league rugby is much more impressive than away, but there was a time where the difference in performance levels was hard to explain. Between September 1998 and October 1999, Gloucester played sixteen home games in the Premiership, winning eleven, drawing one, and losing four. To lose fourteen away games in a row over the same period was more than a coincidence. Chris Catling was a regular at full back at the time.

It was mental. We went to West Hartlepool once, scored five tries and still lost. We used to freeze in the last ten minutes every time. I think if someone could have come up with an answer and put it in a bottle we'd have had one each. We had tried all sorts – different build-up, different mental approaches, even different coaches – but when you get on a roll like that, even though it's negative, it's hard to break out of it. Philippe was really the man who changed things. When we finished third in his first year, we played a simple game, with Simon Mannix kicking for territory a lot and playing the ball into the corners. Once we'd broken the run at Northampton, people believed we could win away.

The run was Gloucester's worst since the Courage League began in 1987, yet during it they managed to reach the final of the now defunct Cheltenham & Gloucester Trophy with a win at National League side Waterloo. That left them to beat Bedford to become the inaugural winners, and although the final wasn't at Kingsholm, it enabled John Brain to put a different spin on how the team might lift the trophy.

The game was on a neutral ground, so to us there was no away bogey to overcome. Philippe wanted the players to show collective responsibility, but by that he didn't mean the team had to play fifteen-man rugby. His vision was a system where everybody knows their job, and positions 9 and 10 run the game. In France players would train and socialise together, so when they go out and play together there is a strong bond. He wanted to bring that bond here.

Brain played in the 1990 cup final defeat by Bath at Twickenham, and Ian Smith, who made his 200th appearance for Gloucester that afternoon, felt the home advantage wasn't as exaggerated in his heyday as it is now.

I've always said that Gloucester people want to see players working as hard on a Saturday as they do during the week. It's the performance they want. They want to see you trying, smashing people about, and if they don't see that, then they point you out. How you won was almost irrelevant. I never used to think about this home and away balance, in fact I used to actually prefer away games if we weren't playing well. The Shed weren't shouting abuse at you.

The raw enthusiasm of the Kingsholm supporters, coupled in many instances with a knowledge that belies their one-eyed reputation, sits neatly with the club's distinguished history, and whether it's offering advice to players or referees, they remain one of the most passionate sets of rugby followers in England. It's a mix that made the ground Don Caskie's favourite venue.

If you were honest and down to earth the fans would take to you. That's why Jake Boer is so popular now. He'd be the equivalent of a John Gadd from my time. A few haven't settled and if they don't fit into the team ethos, the supporters soon pick it up. If you were taking on a Bath or a Leicester, it was the only place to play.

The acid test for Gloucester now is to change their outdated venue without losing the ambience that every former player speaks so highly about. You won't find many of the prawn sandwich clan inside Kingsholm, but a hardy bunch whose prime demands have been a pre-match pint and somewhere (preferably dry) to stand and watch the game. The first drawings done for a potential new site showed four separate stands of equal elevation, three of them seated, with a covered terrace similar to the Shed on the fourth side, but since then ideas have changed, and the layout of the Kingsholm plot would make that plan unworkable. For the new season, clubs have to provide a minimum capacity of 8,200 (which must include 4,000 seats) or have a capacity of 11,000. Clubs who have the higher capacity – of which Gloucester are one – do not have minimum seating requirements at this stage. However, the projected criteria by 2007 shows a need for all clubs to have a 12,000 capacity, of which 4,800 must be seated. The latest strategy assumes Gloucester stay put, and although the Shed may still exist, its form may change according to managing director Ken Nottage.

Modern hero: flanker Jake Boer. (www.gpaimages.com)

Kingsholm development, 2004 style. Phase one shows the new main stand. (Bruce Seabrook/ www.gpaimages.com)

The development plan we have is in two phases, and phase two would be the remodelling of the Shed and the Worcester Street end with a cantilever-type terrace. Phase one involves the main grandstand. Our initial idea shows a new stand running the full length of the pitch, with seating at the rear and terracing for 2,000 in front, and the least scary figure we have had for that is £6 million. We've launched the share issue solely to help with phase one. It would be outstanding if we could raise £2 million, though it's more likely to be £1.5 million, and for that Tom (Walkinshaw) would give up part of his ownership of the club. The difficulty we have is that we are a very public organisation. People are interested and everybody has a view. The work could be done over one summer but it may be that some preparatory work has to be done the previous spring. I'd like to push a button now and see it come out of the ground but my view is that we will be as we are for this season.

Kingsholm's history is rich. The site was chosen from the three under consideration when the club moved from the Spa in 1891 after ruining the playing area they shared with the cricket club by applying salt to it to enable a match against Swansea to go ahead. The seven-acre plot was bought for £4,400, and the first match was staged on 10 October 1891, when Gloucester defeated Burton on Trent by a score of 18-0. Within a decade, the ground staged its first international between England and Wales, and representative games have been a regular occurrence in the century since. Wartime internationals were also staged on Kingsholm, and the ground was one of only three club venues to host a match at the 1991 World Cup between New Zealand and the USA Eagles. Interestingly, the gate takings for that first match were £46 7s 3d – not enough to get two adults into the grandstand this season – and the money to buy the ground came partly from a mortgage, and partly from a share issue. Clearly the old ideas are the best when it comes to raising funds for ground development.

MONEY AND
THE AUTHORITIES

You can't have fifty-seven old ***** *running rugby*

Will Carling's now infamous opinion of the management of rugby union may have been uttered in an off-guard moment, but the authorities have had a lot to answer for in the professional era. Structured seasons, salary caps and central payments have all been regular topics at the top table since the game went open in May 1996, and while the clubs, including Gloucester, have tried to have their input into how the game is run, in some instances they have been left to react to decisions over which they have little or no control. The questions have been coming faster than the answers.

It is perhaps fortunate from Gloucester's point of view that current managing director Ken Nottage has probably sat in on more board meetings of EFDR (now called Premier Rugby) than anyone else. He joined Newcastle in April 1996, and moved to Kingsholm in the summer of 1999, taking over from Hamish Brown. He's also involved in an advisory group within Premier Rugby which looks at the 'selling' of the game from a central point, in an attempt to bring that knowledge back to Kingsholm.

Knowledge though, was not in abundance in 1996. When his boss at Newcastle, Sir John Hall, was driving the top clubs through the gates of professionalism with a formula that had brought success at Newcastle United, others were drawn in. The formula was not right for everyone, but some clubs took on a 'quiet' stance, and didn't acknowledge the implications. Stress, for them, was on the horizon, and that included Gloucester, who didn't have a backer. Successful in an amateur environment, Gloucester were not making enough of a surplus to carry the costs of a professional set-up, and money problems were becoming very real.

Part of the issue in those early days was how the season was planned. The size of the Premiership seems now settled at twelve teams, and the tense finish to last season with regard to relegation suggests that is a good number to sustain interest throughout, but that hasn't always been so. The 1995/96 campaign saw a top division of ten clubs, it then rose to twelve, and for one season (1998/99) was increased again to fourteen, giving each team twenty-six league matches. It's now back to twelve. Moreover, decisions weren't clean. Even at Christmas 1996, Gloucester were unsure how many teams were going down at the end of the season. Team secretary John Fidler saw it as unacceptable to relegate a third of the division, and skipper Dave Sims felt it was better to stick with a dozen teams at the top level. There was a balance to be struck between having too many gaps in the fixture list and lessening the pressure cooker atmosphere the league was now creating.

The players, though, were just pawns in the game. The clubs had to run themselves as never before, and the steer for it all was at the centre. The RFU keep the gate money from the Twickenham internationals, but in other ways their influence helps the clubs. The selling of television rights and sponsorship for the Premiership and the Six Nations is done centrally, and when the money comes into the Union, it then goes via Premier Rugby to the clubs themselves. When the game went open in May 1996, clubs were promised a £500,000 payment from the Union at the start of the following season, but it arrived three months late. Moreover, Gloucester had only four home league games before Christmas. It was the same story a year later and Board chairman David Foyle was distinctly unhappy.

We were not prepared to put up with another fixture list like that. It wasn't fair on the supporters or our bank manager. The fixtures seemed to have been organised by people with very little sense. I thought we needed the majority of the league matches before Christmas, with the cup and the Six Nations afterwards, plus the balance of the league programme. At that stage the fixtures were weighted towards the end of the season. You got the same number of games in the end but it was very lopsided. We were trying to attract new supporters and it was very difficult. I felt the RFU had to listen to the clubs or it would make a joke of the professional game.

Gloucester had Tom Walkinshaw on board by this stage, and he, in his time as the chairman of Premier Rugby, became one of the strongest forces in formulating a blueprint for rugby alongside the Union. At club level, however, he was as a vital cog in Gloucester's cashflow. Problems continued to persist in terms of getting money through from the RFU, and Ken Nottage constantly found himself asking Walkinshaw to prop things up, but that may now be a thing of the past. This season sees phased monthly payments from Premier Rugby to the clubs, irrespective of the flow of funds from the RFU. Moreover, after losing more than £3 million over four seasons, Gloucester's latest accounts also show a small profit. This season's business plan shows no input from Tom Walksinshaw at all, leaving managing director Ken Nottage feeling the Cherry & Whites are making real progress.

The success Gloucester has experienced has been down to Tom Walkinshaw. He will not be able to recoup the money he has put in, but to make the club the best in Europe, and to come here knowing it doesn't cost him anything any more is where his dream lies. He always said when it had its own momentum he would give it back to the fans, and the share issue is the first element of that. Leicester, Northampton and Gloucester have now reported profits, and in my opinion we are the three clubs who are close to not needing a backer.

My simple maths tells me that means nine teams are still losing money, despite interest in the game being at its highest-ever level, and clubs having an imposed salary cap of £1.8 million. In terms of 'back of an envelope' accounting, that money equates to the share each club (including Gloucester) receives from the RFU kitty, as far as it can be guaranteed. There is also a pot at Twickenham for potential extra revenue which can be distributed later, but that's not to be gambled on. However, the question remains as to how clubs can make losses if their first-team squad's salaries are effectively being paid by an outside source. The answer, at least at Kingsholm, appears to be in how they get onto

Kingsholm managing director Ken Nottage.
(www.gpaimages.com)

the field. Gloucester's support staff to the first-team squad cost them close to £1 million last season. That total includes all the coaching and medical staff, plus the administrative back up. It's a frightening figure, and one the club must reduce before a salary cap in this area is also imposed by the RFU for the start of next season.

The £1.8 million salary cap for players was introduced for the start of the 1999/2000 season at a time when rugby's off-the-field discussions were at their most intense. It was appropriate because the sport itself was in danger of overheating, partly due to the enthusiasm of club owners when the game went professional. Even average players found themselves being very well rewarded, and while the salary cap gave clubs a crutch to lean on, the players were getting themselves into the mix via the new PRA, an association formed by the players at the Premiership clubs.

By the summer of 2001, five seasons after the lifting of the moratorium, and three years after the clubs really started stamping their feet about the way the game was being run, agreement was finally reached on all sides about the way forward. Gloucester's player representative until the summer of 2003 was Chris Catling.

The season as it is now came about because (outside World Cup years) we can't move the European Cup or the internationals, and the only thing we had any power over was the Premiership. The PRA was a good mix, including Tim Stimpson from Leicester and John Phillips from Northampton. We weren't all internationals, and we were aware we were arguing our corner for the whole profession, and that included things like welfare and benefit issues. We felt we needed to address things earlier than had been done in the past, because rugby had been guilty of doing things far too late – halfway through a season we'd still be talking about relegation rules and qualification for Europe. One of our big talking points was not having more than one game a week. Fans don't want to see tired players, and that's when injuries occur. It was a partnership, and we thought the deal as a whole was excellent.

Tom Walkinshaw was Premier Rugby chairman at the time the agreement was finalised.

Everyone bought into it because we felt it was better to have an industry where you could look at a long-term career rather than have a windfall profit for a couple of years and then be on the dole. It was a true joint venture between the Union, the clubs and the players, and we went to great lengths to ensure the right financial environment could be created. Everyone was getting an agreed percentage on the 'off' side of the game, and international players were limited to thirty-two matches per season. It was the first time proper foundations had been set down to manage and develop the game at club and international level.

One of the key decisions that was made in Walkinshaw's time as chairman was the introduction of the end of season play-offs. There is little doubt in my view that it is purely a money-making exercise, and that actually it isn't steered by the sponsors, but by the clubs themselves, as the beneficiaries are not just the finalists, but the whole of the division. The first season they were introduced, the crowd of 33,500 for Leicester's 22-10 win over Bath justified the concept. Gloucester, having finished seventh, were drawn away to runners-up Wasps in the first round and lost 18-6. Twelve months later they were to finish the season in style.

At that time the Premiership and the play-offs were separate. If there was any doubt as to who should be truly called the champions, Leicester avoided any argument in that first season by winning both. By the spring of 2002, the Tigers had again proved their durability to secure the title, so it was a surprise when in wet and muddy conditions they lost to Bristol, in so doing relinquishing their long unbeaten record against English teams

Players' rep: Chris Catling was
Gloucester's PRA man until he joined
Beziers in 2003. (www.gpaimages.com)

at Welford Road. If their motivation wasn't quite at 100 per cent, it opened a door of opportunity for others.

Gloucester, third in the final table, were left to face Newcastle at home – a thorny little fixture after what had happened at Kingsholm on 29 December 2001. Olivier Azam and Epi Taione didn't display much Christmas cheer to each other, both were sent off, and allegations of racism emerged from the Falcons' director of rugby, Rob Andrew. Gloucester undertook a full enquiry, and found no evidence of racial abuse, and the match report of referee Roy Maybank didn't mention anything either. It took three months for the matter to be resolved, despite repeated calls from Gloucester for Andrew to apologise. In the end Gloucester made their point in the best way possible, rattling up nine tries in a 60-9 victory, much to the delight of new director of rugby Nigel Melville.

We sent Newcastle home with a flea in their ear. We were a bit casual to start with but when we tightened up we created the gaps and took our chances. I looked along the line in the second half as the ball was coming out, and who's on the end of it but Vicks. A prop on the left wing! The fact he went round one and through a number of others to score was probably why he was man of the match.

The Gloucester captain was delighted to finish the season at Kingsholm with such a big win.

It was a fantastic day. The Rob Andrew thing got the crowd going and they had a bit of fun with him but as an incident it was something we needed to forget and move forward – which we did. That result meant we had scored 50 points for three games in a row, so we had to remember why we had done it when we went to Sale for the semi-final. They're a good all-round side – Angelsea, Pinkerton, Hodgson, Redpath, they're all good players – and you're only as good as your last game. The motivation was to get to the final.

Sale paraded the Parker Pen Shield to their supporters before the match, but having lost to the Sharks in the semi-final, Gloucester didn't fancy a repeat. A try by Tom Beim against his former club helped the Cherry & Whites ease through 33-11, and with Bristol beating Northampton, the final would be a West Country derby played out over 200 times before. It would also be their fourth meeting of the season, and Vickery acknowledged that to beat the same side four times was very difficult.

Mentally a final is a big occasion and you have to make sure your top two inches are right and that you take care of your own responsibilities. After the Heineken semi-final I got quite a lot of stick from supporters, so it was nice then to get to a final.

Flanker Jake Boer agreed a win would be a fine way to cap the season.

We had had a good run, Nigel had changed a few things and it had been positive towards the players. We had achieved our goals as regards a league place, and then we had the final as well.

How about that? Phil Vickery celebrates his try against Newcastle. (www.gpaimages.com)

Bristol had looked sharp in the semi-final, but we hoped we would put pressure on Contepomi and Pichot and hopefully force some errors.

Boer was be Gloucester's solitary try scorer on the day, but the metronomic boot of Mercier kept totting up the points as Bristol's penalty count rose steadily throughout the match. Mercier kicked seven in all, enough to give Gloucester a 28-23 victory and Nigel Melville his first piece of silverware barely three months after arriving at Kingsholm.

Flanker Jake Boer touches down at Twickenham. (www.gpaimages.com)

I was just so pleased it ended the way it did. It was never going to be an open, flowing game and we gave a cheap try away which didn't help. We saw what it means to win at Gloucester, and if anyone was ever in any doubt, believe me it's important. You only had to look at Vicks in the dressing room beforehand. He's a big game player – and it showed.

Bristol lost more than the match that day. Director of rugby Dean Ryan soon left to join Nigel Melville at Gloucester, and throughout last season the threat of relegation never seemed far away. What happened on the final weekend, with Bath beating Newcastle, and Bristol losing at London Irish, neatly solved (from the RFU's viewpoint) any political issues that may have arisen from a merger between them and Bath, but it also emphasised the gulf financially between the Premiership and anything else. Bristol were relegated after finishing bottom of the table. They lost virtually a full squad, forcing them to rebuild almost from scratch, and their income from the RFU for this season is merely a parachute payment of around £700,000. Added complications regarding possible promotion back to the Premiership also include insufficient seats at the Memorial Ground and primacy of tenure over the venue. It looks unlikely they will make an immediate return, and it raises questions about what happens to the side that finishes bottom at the end of this season.

The one thing we do know is that they will be relegated, because the chief executive of the RFU, Francis Baron, used his casting vote to pass the motion in favour of direct promotion and relegation rather than a play-off system. It was a decision that would have been welcomed at clubs like Worcester and a resurgent Orrell, but not at Gloucester. The reason concerns the club's need for additional investment, as Ken Nottage explains.

I was really deflated by that decision because it threatens our very future. It is difficult for us to convince a financial institution to lend us money while the threat of relegation exists. It puts a massive hurdle in front of us. A play-off is much easier for us because the club outside the Premiership has to carry a squad of a high standard for a whole season, and there is still an element of doubt about going up at the end of it. You would have to have substantial reserves to do that.

The money Gloucester need, as has been well documented, is for the redevelopment of Kingsholm. Unlike other sports, rugby doesn't have a grant aid system through a body the equivalent, for example, of the Football Trust, which helped Cheltenham Town to the tune of nearly £1 million when they built a new stand in 2001. Gloucester have to find all the money themselves, and despite what I believe is a fairly relaxed attitude at this stage towards ground criteria from the Union, it's hard to see that remaining so if Gloucester's facilities audit for the next two years is unchanged. You really do get the impression that the club's progress has now got to a point where is it being hampered by the facilities. The bare facts are these. The ground was, on average, 86 per cent full for all home games last season. For league games alone, the spare capacity was less than 4 per

Au revoir: Olivier Azam (left) and Ludovic Mercier after their last game at Kingsholm. (www.gpaimages.com)

cent. It's not unreasonable to assume that with some people being turned away from games that were sold out, the seasonal average could well have been higher than the current 11,000 capacity of Kingsholm. Ken Nottage accepts the current graph would be at the top of its arc.

It won't get much better than last season. We made a small profit and we won a major trophy, but to take the club to the next level, we must generate more profit. What happens on the pitch is the driver for everything. You get a successful team and sponsors, corporate guests and regular fans want to be part of it. If Kingsholm stays as it is, the best we hope for is the same as last season, but we want to make the club bigger and better, so that we can put more money into all areas. The ground is the biggest stumbling block to that – and the team has to be as good at the same time.

That's not an easy compromise to evaluate, and the value for money equation was a recurring one at Kingsholm throughout last season. The spark for it was two major business interests of backer Tom Walkinshaw, the Arrows Formula 1 team and his TWR group, which had been in existence for twenty-seven years, going into receivership and administration respectively. The populist conclusion was that Gloucester would also be in trouble, and the loss of French prop Patrice Collazo to Toulouse in September 2002 was seen as evidence of that. Collazo, however, was near the top of Gloucester's payroll, and by allowing him to leave when he did, they were able to recruit and register Rodrigo Roncero in time for the start of the Heineken Cup. I think it is common knowledge that the salaries of the two men weren't the same. Stories regarding players not being paid on time, and then being asked to take pay cuts came and went. Ken Nottage acknowledged all wasn't well, but the illness wasn't terminal.

There was pain in the process but we were looking for a better result at the end. Cuts were made in all areas, and there have been casualties through natural wastage. The costs are more than the players, they exceeded the income and that's what we needed to adjust. Pretty much all the clubs would have been going through this process because the money from the RFU central funding was significantly down from the initial figures. The early indications were that it could be about £2.7 million, considerably more than the £1.8 million for the salary cap, but the commercial side became increasingly difficult and everyone had to balance their books accordingly.

To borrow a line from Keith Richardson earlier in the book, Gloucester is a club that weathers storms. Last season off the field, life was blustery for a while, but the end result financially was a better than break even situation. It did appear however, that there would be one or two sacrificial lambs at the end of it, and it was no surprise when Mercier and Azam followed Collazo back to France. The recruiting of four players to cover the ten departures shows rationalisation, and awareness that overspending is no longer an option, and having invested in an Academy, the club knows it must produce more players such as Marcel Garvey who are capable of playing regular first-team rugby. A sort of 'home-grown' solution – just like it used to be.

SHEDHEADS

The period covered by this book starts and ends with two cup finals. Gloucester took in excess of 20,000 supporters to the final in 1990, and around 30,000 to the 2003 final against Northampton, but clearly a large number of those spectators are 'casual' supporters. Crowds at Kingsholm have grown in the intervening years, as has the number of outlets that feed them. In 1990, their first port of call would have been *The Citizen* or the two local radio stations. Internet technology was still in the future, and there was no *Shedhead* magazine to give an off-beat view of Kingsholm life. There wasn't even an official supporters club. The pace of change since has been rapid.

The obvious event to kick start it all was rugby going professional, but not all supporters have the same demands. While some will access all areas for the merest snippet of information, for others rugby is not the drug of everyday life, but where things have changed is over the rights of supporters, particularly if you have been a season-ticket holder at Gloucester for more than a decade. The AGM was held annually in July, and season-ticket holders, as members, were allowed to attend. Those who so wished would criticise the committee, and if the feeling was strong enough, the voting would dictate changes. Clubs having majority shareholders, however, altered all that, and independent groups on a local and national level were formed. Gloucester's is the GRSA, the Gloucester Rugby Supporters Association. It came into existence in the summer of 1999, and has a membership of over 700. The current treasurer is Alistair Thomson.

A number of us got together when there was talk of Tom Walkinshaw's stake in the club going up from 73 per cent to 98 per cent because there was concern that the average supporter who regularly bought his season ticket wouldn't have a voice any more. We are an independent, properly

OPPOSITE ABOVE:
Peter Tocknell, from the STSA presents the association's Player of the Year Award 2002/03 to Jake Boer. (www.gpaimages.com)

LEFT:
John Neary, chairman of the National Rugby Supporters Association.

constituted company, and the value of that was shown with the Rob Andrew affair. We went to our members and said we had decided to take legal action, whereas the Season Ticket Holders Association decided not to. We knew that apart from the directors, if it all went pear shaped each and every member would only be liable for £1. Both organisations are supporting the same club, but the Rob Andrew situation was a classic example of why it would be great if we could have one supporter's body – one that was supportive, but independent.

The three elements that were pulled together to form GRSA were the regular supporters who travelled to away games, the readers of the popular and irreverent *Shedhead* fanzine, and the growing number of internet friendly supporters who accessed the *Kingsholm Chronicle* website. Their relationship with the club has on the whole been supportive, but there have been one or two niggles along the way, including a period when the association's page in the match-day programme was stopped after the club was criticised. Leeds Tykes is the latest Premiership side to form such an independent association, and there's a national one too, where the chairman, John Neary, also happens to be a Gloucester supporter, and he feels the word independent is crucial.

We all love the club, and every organisation has a different method for getting what they want but in my opinion you must have a degree of independence because otherwise you will come down on the club's side all the time because they are what you might call the paymasters. GRSA are independent, whereas the Season Ticket Holders Association doesn't have an elected committee but a committee appointed by the club. It's a sop really. It can work with an independent body, as we have shown at a national level. The National Rugby Supporters Association now meets regularly with both the RFU and Premier Rugby, and it's got to a stage where they send us every bit of information that is circulated to the media.

Such co-operation over the flow of information is of course, healthy, and the flow for most fans at Gloucester is through the STHA, which this season bears its new name, the Cherry & White Members Club. You automatically become a member once you have purchased a season ticket, and its formation came after the apathy at the turnstiles that greeted the large rise in admission prices in the summer of 1998. Gloucester felt they needed a filter between themselves and the supporters, and the STHA was born. Season ticket rates and ground development have been regular topics of conversation since, with chairman Terry Short invited to attend rugby club board meetings when specific agenda items are to be raised. One of his committee members is Peter Tocknell.

We discuss a lot of things and while we cannot release everything, sometimes I think we are a bit behind the times in letting people know what is going on. A media representative is one of our ideas for the new season. It would be nice to have just one supporters' body, and people within the GRSA have come to us with points to be put forward because they are active members of both organisations. The level of season tickets has increased markedly in the last couple of years but that is because the club has been successful. People want to come and watch a good side but you have to ask what will happen if we don't do so well for the next season or two. We have quite a small catchment area and as a percentage of population Gloucester has a good following, but the real hard-core support could be as low as between 3,000 and 5,000.

It's a point well made. Gloucester's league attendances barely averaged 5,000 as recently as 1996/97, and they were still under 7,000 during the first year in the Heineken Cup (2000/01), but you sense the core support will become stronger the longer the team keep winning. That's how Bath built their fan base in the 1980s and 1990s, and you also feel the matches mean more to supporters now than ever before. Graham Spring is in his twenty-sixth season as PA announcer at Kingsholm. His only roles at his first match were to read out the teams and give out the winner of the £1 prize for the lucky programme number at half-time, but he feels the supporter's package has changed for the better since then.

To me these are the greatest days to be a Gloucester supporter, and it isn't just because of the success on the field. Friendlies don't exist any more and the game is ten times better for it. I believe every one of the 11,000 supporters has far more passion in what the club does now than ever they did years ago, even though they may not all admit it. I felt as if the world had ended when we lost to Bath in the 1990 final. The dislike of Bath and the will to beat them now is based on memories. We'd been so close so often, and every time it was them that stopped us (1985, 1989, 1992 and 1996), but now there are more things to go for than just the cup. It's great we're back to full houses again. I can remember playing two home games over Easter against New Brighton and Birkenhead Park and you would be lucky to get 3,000 for each match. Just that we're getting 11,000 proves that the passion is there and that people want Gloucester to be the top club.

It's a passion that comes through in both the supporters' bodies associated with the club, although the new Cherry & White members club is the one with the official stamp. It has the direct access up the chain within the club, but concerns over its representation

Kingsholm's microphone
man Graham Spring.
(www.gpaimages.com)

remain for the likes of Bob Fenton. Fenton and Ed Snow were the founders of the *Shedhead* fanzine in 1995, an inexpensive and sideways look at all things Gloucester, and a vehicle to put what a lot of fans were thinking into print. Fenton is a season-ticket holder and a member of GRSA, but isn't alone in thinking that just one of them should be enough.

The ideal would be a meeting of minds and a merger between the two. I think you can have an independent association which can bring the club to account on certain things without having a confrontational relationship. I can't affect the running of the Cherry & White members club because I don't have a democratic right. It was unfortunate the club set up the STHA because by name it's exclusive. People who attend regularly but who can't afford to pay up front for a season ticket, or who live away and maybe go to a lot of the games near London and only come to a handful of home games have no representation, and situations where club officials or players are actively stopped from going to GRSA meetings is unhealthy. All we want is a successful club and a good relationship between the club and the fans.

The historical caricature of the Gloucester supporter is an interesting one. The mental philosophy, as Andy Deacon intimated, was that the rest of the world was against you. Referees and the RFU don't like you, and neither did the England management, who tended to pick players from their 'favourite' clubs. You expected hard graft, were a bit on the miserable side, and consequently when the side did win, you were prone to be a bit over the top. Gradually however, the balance is shifting, though I'm sure there is an element that is never happier than when it's moaning. Tim Holder has been a regular supporter beside the players' tunnel for more than forty years.

There are a lot of new supporters at Kingsholm who have not been immersed into the rugby culture, either people who have never been before, or people who have moved into the area, and very quickly they have become ardent supporters. Even living in Cinderford you see a good number of Gloucester shirts, and the closer you get to the ground on a match day, the more you see. It makes your blood tingle, and the desire to win has become an expectation. Probably 90 per cent of the crowd would probably prefer to see Gloucester win even if it was a poor game, but there are signs that people are responding to flair as well as the traditional strengths, and let's face it if you can win with style that's a bonus. I don't think the fans care in the least who they watch now. You only have to look at the popularity of Mercier and Azam, both complete strangers, but adopted by the club as if they were their own. They were cult heroes, yet there was no reason why they should have been.

Tim writes his own match reports and this season has launched a website where you can read them (www.gloucestermatches.me.uk). Gloucester is well served by websites, included the one that is a spin off from the *Shedhead* magazine. In its own way *Shedhead* was the start of an improved flow of information and probably brought the players and the supporters closer together, and while he accepts things have moved on since, Bob Fenton is proud to have been associated with it.

At the time there was no vehicle for comment and I think Shedhead *changed opinions. Attention was paid to what fans were thinking, and we would get correspondents like David Hands from* The Times *ringing us. We almost became the litmus paper, a voice on the changes in rugby generally. People forget Richard Hill was the first coach to bring in young foreign players at a time when Gloucester's image was one of an introverted club where anyone from Cheltenham was a foreigner. I remember giving Richard a copy of the first edition of* Shedhead *and he looked at me as if I was mad. Now we exist alongside everything else but there is an over-reliance on electronic technology. Probably only half of our supporters have access to the internet. I pay £155 for my season ticket, and while the club send me sales-related literature a bit more information to me as a supporter wouldn't go amiss.*

Fanzine founders: *Shedhead*'s authors Bob Fenton (right) and Ed Snow at the restored war memorial at Kingsholm.

Tim Holder, a regular fan at
Kingsholm since the 1950s.

Fenton is also a regular traveller to Gloucester's away games, where the camaraderie and reputation of the club's supporters can be seen to the full. Gloucester would probably have a bigger travelling support than anyone in English rugby apart from Leicester, and the numbers who go abroad in the Heineken Cup have grown steadily from the 500 or so who went to Stade Français in 1997. The perception is that they get on well with everyone – no doubt the bar takings help that impression – and messages via e-mail and the web from supporters of other clubs suggest the Gloucester gospel is well received. It's a traditional one as well, as Alistair Thomson explains.

Other clubs are envious of our fan base, and when you go away with Gloucester it's like being at a family party. We're very passionate but what differentiates rugby supporters from football supporters is that the anger and the post mortems aren't as intense. We ARE gutted if we lose but after a couple of pints we're all looking forward to the next match. In Munster, for example, it all went terribly wrong on the pitch but after a couple of drinks it was just the most fantastic place to be.

That atmosphere is something Gloucester fans can look forward to again this season, with Munster and the Cherry & Whites again being drawn in the same group in the Heineken Cup. The home game at Kingsholm is once again certain to be a sell out, and the demand for tickets on such occasions has made the need for Gloucester to have a bigger ground a major talking point. The club have come down on the side of redeveloping their traditional home, and while that might please the majority, a small straw poll here drew a variety of opinions. Graham Spring would have liked to have started afresh and built a new stadium similar to the Madjeski in Reading with a 25,000 capacity, but that worries Bob Fenton, who feels the atmosphere might be dissipated. He would prefer a re-development on Kingsholm to around a 16,000 capacity so that bigger crowds can be accommodated without losing any of the ambience that currently exists. John Neary felt a new ground with other facilities attached, such as a hotel, could have brought vital extra revenue, but that a Northampton style rebuild on Kingsholm would be more than acceptable. Peter Tocknell would prefer the club to stay at Kingsholm because of the history attached to it, and Alistair Thomson, who is an accountant by profession, would like to see Kingsholm's capacity increased with the minimum of investment.

No work is likely to start on this until the spring of 2004 at the earliest, by which time the club will hope the share issue used to fund a percentage of it will have been fully subscribed. The season too will be reaching its climax, a season where the World Cup will have a big impact, and just as over the ground development, views on the prospects are mixed.

John Neary, Gloucester supporter and chairman of the National Rugby Supporters Association.

I'm optimistic. Nigel Melville is a shrewd coach, and we're in the winning mode now. Bath and Leicester have both enjoyed a spell of dominance, maybe it's our turn.

Graham Spring, Kingsholm's PA announcer.

I feel we are not as strong this year as last season, and I see a lot of gaps if we suffer with injuries. Like many, I worry we will lose out because of money. We don't have a Chelsea situation. The game is still evolving, but I'm not sure we are in a better position this year to progress past Munster in the Heineken Cup. Unless we have half a dozen Marcel Garveys coming through I think we're going to slip down the other side of the peak.

Peter Tocknell, committee member of the Cherry & White members club.

It's hard to get to the top and it's harder to stay there. I'd be surprised if we won the league. I'd be happy with a top four finish so that we stay in the Heineken Cup and a good run in the Powergen. I also think we must look after the grass roots. People I talk to still have concerns about what happens in the board room and the club being bank rolled financially.

Tim Holder, a long standing supporter.

I'm not as optimistic as I was last season, probably because of financial constraints, and I'm not sure we'll be good enough for long enough to finish top of the league again.

Bob Fenton, co-founder of *Shedhead*.

Expectations have been raised, and people are talking about a Heineken Cup semi-final as a realistic objective. I'd be surprised if we weren't in contention for major honours. The World Cup will distort the Premiership and clubs like Leeds and Harlequins ought to profit from that. Maybe we ought to look at the Wasps model from last season. They pedalled strongly after Christmas, knowing they couldn't catch us and then beat us in a one-off final. If we did that I don't think you would find too many people knocking the structure, but I feel finishing fourth wouldn't be seen as good enough any more.

Things have come a long way since Richard Hill arrived in 1995 and knocked Gloucester into shape. The aim now, on and off the field, is to take the transition to the next level.

SEMI-FINAL
MISSES

Losing a final isn't the best way to finish a season, but at least you have everything else that goes with it – the build-up, the expectation, and, above all, a day out. Losing a semi-final is an altogether different experience. You are left feeling empty, mentally so near to lifting the trophy, yet in reality no better off than teams eliminated at the first hurdle. Emotionally, for anyone connected with a club that goes through it, from players to administrators and supporters, it's a draining experience, and one Gloucester have needed some thick skin to cope with over the past decade or so.

Between the two finals that provide the bridge for the period of this book, Gloucester reached four knockout cup semi-finals, and lost the lot. I accept they did win two Cheltenham & Gloucester Trophy semi-finals, one at Leicester and one at Waterloo, and a play-off semi-final at Sale in 2002, but when the chips were really down in the Blue Riband competition, they couldn't find the answers. The games were a varied mix, two at home and two away, and two of them were against Bath, who were masters of getting through one way or another, which after all is what semi-finals are all about. It doesn't really matter how you win, so long as you do.

The first disappointment came in 1992. Gloucester had beaten Rugby, London Scottish and Orrell to go through to the semi-final draw, and when the balls were drawn out, number two (Gloucester) was followed by number one (Bath). It was their first meeting in the cup since the 1990 final, and Gloucester had also lost both league meetings since the debacle at Twickenham.

The side was virtually at full strength, but the players had had to cope with two Courage League games the week before, a home fixture against London Irish, and an away trip to Orrell, which had ended in defeat.

Of all the four semi-final failures, this one was probably the most heartbreaking. The match was closely contested throughout, with Dave Sims giving a rousing performance. Bath scored the only try of the first half through wing Jim Fallon, although there was an element of doubt as to whether the ball was grounded properly. Barnes converted and kicked a penalty, but a Neil Matthews dropped goal and two Tim Smith penalties tied the scores at 9-9. Two more Barnes penalties gave Gloucester ground to make up in the last quarter, but Smith, who played well throughout, kicked another penalty and then dropped a goal himself with ten minutes to go.

It was still all square as full time approached, but there was then a crucial incident with Dave Sims being forced to go off with a head injury, much to his annoyance.

I think that was my best game ever for the club. A guy got past me, and as I tackled him I took a bang and knocked myself out. When I came round I had this lump above my eyebrows. I wanted

Defensive duties: Don Caskie leads the tracking of Phil de Glanville (ABOVE) and Simon Morris halts a run by Jim Fallon (BELOW).

to carry on, but when I went and stood in the line-out I had my back to the thrower. I had no choice really when the doctor told me to go off.

It was left to skipper Ian Smith to lift the team for extra time. Tim Smith kicked another penalty in the first period, but just when you thought Bath were a spent force in the face of some determined Gloucester tackling, an error turned the game on its head. Pete Miles, the man who replaced Dave Sims, was part of the team that famously beat Bath four years later in a critical league game at Kingsholm, but as Smith recalls this wasn't such a happy occasion.

Pete slapped the ball back from a line-out near our own line and we had to concede a scrum. Bath won the ball and I think Tony Swift scored, and that started the rot. There wasn't long to go and they got another try after that (scored by Jim Fallon). Any game against Bath was a tremendous affair and a huge challenge, but once you knew how deep you had to dig to beat them it was quite frightening.

Bath's scrum half that day was Richard Hill, and by the time Gloucester got into the last four again, he had stopped playing, left Bath, and come to Kingsholm as director of rugby. The gap between the two ties was four years, but Gloucester still had three survivors from the 1992 defeat – centre Don Caskie, lock Dave Sims, who was now captain, and his predecessor Ian Smith. Bath, interestingly, had eight. They were also protecting an astonishing cup record, having lifted the cup nine times in twelve seasons, thereby proving that there is a knack to winning semi-finals.

The Rec, a ground of much misery for Gloucester and their supporters.

You shall not pass: wing Mike Peters is held up by the Bath defence.

Fate was always likely to pair the two clubs together in the draw, and although this time it was Bath who had home advantage, Hill wasn't fazed about going back to the Rec.

Bath got big crowds but it was a fair-weather support. People would go and watch internationals and a winning team. Before they had success, Bath didn't get big crowds. Gloucester has a hard-core support and I remember running out on the Rec and hearing the 'Glawster' chant.

It was support that was in evidence again as Gloucester sought to topple the cup favourites. After wins over Walsall, Notttingham and Wasps in the earlier rounds, much of the debate in the build-up had concerned the selection of Mark Mapletoft at full back. He'd been sidelined by injury for over a year, and Gloucester hadn't had the chance to play him in a truly competitive game since his return to action against the Army barely a fortnight earlier. Critically, he was to miss two kickable penalties in the second half.

Gloucester's problems in the first half were largely of their own making, and they were repeatedly pulled up for infringements by referee Ed Morrison. Jon Callard kicked three early penalties, and added a fourth just before half-time. Gloucester's only points had come from a Martyn Kimber dropped goal and they failed to build momentum in any area of play. Neither side had managed a try at the change round but Bath made a devastating start to the second half through Adedayo Adebayo, who skated in for a try from the halfway line having broken a tackle by Mike Peters. Callard's conversion made it 19-3, but thereafter it was all Gloucester. Quick thinking by Benton saw him snatch a try which Mapletoft converted, but a missed dropped goal by Kimber and some wayward kicking from Mapletoft meant chances were spurned. Long spells of pressure brought no reward and lock Rob Fidler accepted the first 20 minutes were crucial.

Bath had thirteen internationals and we respected them a bit too much early on. Callard would kick penalties from anywhere if he's within range, we gave them away and that didn't help. We may not have had the depth in the squad that they did, but you put on the Gloucester shirt and it does raise your game a level or two. If only we'd gone at them in the first half like we did in the second.

Richard Hill felt Gloucester's performance showed that progress was being made.

Our second half was wonderful. There weren't many teams who could play Bath at the Rec and ensure a quiet dressing room afterwards. We spoke about penalties beforehand and then went and gave three away. Our penalties came from pressure and we missed them. Bath had pace and their defence was good but 19-10 wasn't a fair reflection.

The tenacity and spirit Gloucester showed at the Rec was the defining characteristic of his early times as director of rugby. While others were recruiting foreign stars as the game went open, Hill was straining every ounce out of a solely home-based squad. The disappointment at the Rec pushed them on the following season, but this semi-final didn't come at an ideal time. Once again, injuries couldn't really be blamed. Eleven of the side that had lost at Bath were still prominent members of the squad, but form had become patchy once the winning streak in the league had been broken at Bristol. Gloucester had entered the cup in the fifth round, and aided by 30 points from Mark Mapletoft, they beat Leeds 55-20, showing them they still had some ground to make up against Premiership opposition. A favourable draw in the last sixteen saw Bristol come to Kingsholm, where a typically sharp second-half try by Scott Benton was finally enough to ease them out 18-12. The thought of a repeat of previous horrors at Wakefield loomed large once the quarter-final draw was clear cut, but Gloucester did just enough against their National League opponents, Mike Peters scoring the only try in open play in a 25-21 win that put Gloucester into the last four alongside Harlequins, Leicester and Sale.

All three were above Gloucester in the Courage League, so a home draw – albeit against Leicester – wasn't the worst possible option. Gloucester hadn't been beaten at home in the league or the cup since September. Mapletoft was now at fly half, with Chris Catling having established himself at full back. Only four of the team beaten at the Rec a year earlier weren't selected, among them Don Caskie, with Richard Hill breaking up his partnership with Martin Roberts at centre in order to include the inexperienced but fleet of foot Craig Emmerson.

I make the point about home-based players because the match-winner at Kingsholm that day was a South African. Joel Stransky had considerable international experience, and displayed a cool head when it was needed. The Tigers, still playing in their traditional letters, had four penalty chances in the first 12 minutes. Stransky, wearing the letter J given to the outside half, kicked three of them and Gloucester were chasing the game having hardly been into Leicester territory. It was a carbon copy of what had happened against Bath, even to the point that the half-time score was also the same – 12-3 after Mapletoft registered his first successful kick of the afternoon. Gradually Gloucester's backs started to threaten, and Emmerson justified his selection with a fine break. Catling supported him and as he strove for the line, the pack powered through in support to drive the full back the final few metres to score. Mapletoft converted and traded penalties with Stransky. A bit like apprentices learning their trade, Gloucester then lost out to the more streetwise side at the death, but you wonder what would have happened had Mark Mapletoft slotted a dropped goal chance. He certainly does.

If I had been playing at 10 longer, my first instinct might have been to go for the drop, but the split second I took to decide was critical. Stransky had three goes and two of them went over, one of them from static ball 40 metres out. At 13-15 we had every chance but they put us to the sword in the end and the score totted up. It was a pity because that was the best we had played for about two months.

The last word: Richard Hill issues instructions before kick off against Leicester.

Those two Stransky dropped goals came in the last ten minutes, ruining all Gloucester's hard work in the second half. Steve Hackney's try merely confirmed Leicester's place in the final, leaving Gloucester still without a cup semi-final win at Kingsholm in four attempts. It's a record that still stands, and Richard Hill saw Leicester's greater experience as a big influence.

We were very eager and our bug was that we did concede a lot of penalties. Before you knew it, it was 9-0 and it's difficult to recover. We were criticised for not having strike runners but we cut them apart at times and I thought we played the better rugby in the three quarters. Unfortunately John Brain and I had mentioned about not throwing to the back of the line-out because Simon Devereux was getting a nudge, but we kept on doing it and Steve Lander wasn't spotting it. The crowd kept us going but you can't knock Stransky. He's a good player, Leicester relied on him and they did well to win.

It was to be Hill's last tilt at a semi-final with Gloucester. They were unceremoniously dumped out at Northampton the following year, and although they were still involved in February 1999, with a home quarter-final against Harlequins looming, that wasn't enough for him to keep his job. Almost inevitably, given that quarter-final came in what is colloquially known as the 'honeymoon' period after a change of coach, Gloucester squeezed through to set up a semi-final against Wasps, who were by now playing at Loftus Road. It was now up to Philippe Saint-André to try and break this losing run at the last hurdle.

The former French captain had been in charge at Kingsholm for barely six weeks when the semi-final came round. He was still picking himself to play despite his new responsibilities, and with a need for an accurate goal kicker, he accommodated Mark Mapletoft in the team on the opposite wing rather than at outside half, where it was felt Simon Mannix was better suited defensively to Wasps tactics. For Dave Sims, selected as a replacement, it was a fourth semi-final, while Mapletoft, Deacon and captain for the day Rob Fidler hoped it would be third time lucky. On form, having lost every away game in the league since September, Wasps were hot favourites, but Saint-André didn't mind that.

I am French and I liked being the outsider. We had to play with heart and spirit but also I had to change the mentality. We had scored five tries to two at West Hartlepool and yet the penalty count was 25-5 and we lost. The discipline wasn't good enough, and we didn't play enough collective rugby. When you are eighty minutes from Twickenham, you must have a good collective to win.

It wasn't a skill Gloucester displayed to any great degree on that Easter Sunday afternoon. Of the four semi-final defeats, this was the most one-sided. Gloucester's cohesion in midfield was poor and their threat of a try was minimal. It was left to the boot of Mapletoft to keep them in the game for much of the match, and approaching half-time the Cherry & Whites actually led 12-9, thanks to a Sanders dropped goal and three Mapletoft penalties. There was also an element of doubt over a possible try for Fanolua,

Top view: the packed hospitality boxes watch as Rob Fidler contests a line-out.

but Wasps stung Gloucester either side of the interval. First Gloucester lost a line-out on their own ball, and Rob Henderson strolled through to score, and then Ed Pearce failed to control the ball at the rear of a scrum, allowing Paul Sampson to gather and burst through three tackles to touch down. Two Logan conversions, added to his earlier penalties, gave Wasps an eleven-point lead and they never looked back. Mapletoft kept Gloucester in touch with three more penalties, but in between Wasps flanker Paul Volley got a try after a rolling maul, and Logan had the last word with a try which he converted himself. Gloucester forwards coach John Brain accepted that four tries to nil was a comprehensive defeat.

We found it hard to breach their defence, and when we made mistakes they punished us. We picked Mark on the wing because he was too good to leave out and we thought it might wrong foot Wasps, but the try on half-time was the killer blow, especially when you lose a line-out on halfway and they score under the posts. The other key point was just after it at 16-12. Mark misses a penalty to make it 16-15, and they go up the other end and score and it's 23-12. In the end though, we couldn't argue.

Kingsley Jones, who was to captain the side the following season, watched the match from the stands because of injury.

Bombed out: Simon Mannix (ABOVE) and Steve Ojomoh (OPPOSITE ABOVE) struggle to make any headway through the Wasps cover.

We did well in the first half but we had a problem in taking chances. If we had taken them it might have been different, but in the second half Wasps deserved it. They lived off scraps at times but every good opportunity they had, they finished it off. The whole team was committed but it's still very disappointing.

Why some teams do better in semi-finals than others is hard to fathom, particularly when their merits are on a par. Dave Sims claims that Gloucester's record in the Cheltenham & Gloucester Trophy proved they didn't have a problem with semi-finals, but I would argue that wasn't at the same level as, for example, a tie in the last four of the Powergen or Heineken Cup. An association of ideas can play a part mentally, and I've no doubt that just as Gloucester got into the losing habit away from Kingsholm at one stage, to record a string of wins at home helps them as much in a positive sense when they play in front of their own fans. In their pomp, Bath never expected to lose a semi-final once they got there, and ahead of the 1996 semi-final against Gloucester, the local paper even printed details of ticket and coach arrangements for the final on the Friday before the match. As Ben Curtis showed at the 2003 Open Golf Championship, some rookies don't choke when the pressure is on, but experience will generally stand you in good stead. In each of these four semi-finals, Gloucester's blend wasn't quite right, and they came up short, while in his time as Wasps, Nigel Melville's record in semi-finals was good, winning three, and then going on to lift the cup on two occasions. It was a record the Cherry & White fans hoped would continue when Melville joined Gloucester.

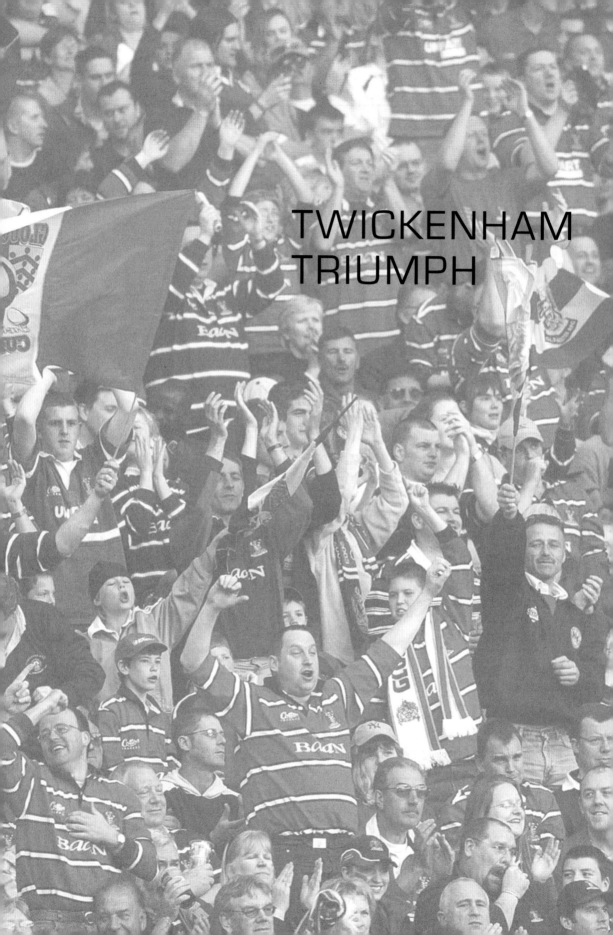

TWICKENHAM
TRIUMPH

CLASSIC MATCH 7

5 April 2003, Twickenham, Pilkington Cup (Final)
Gloucester 40 Northampton 22

Gloucester put in a display of fervour and passion to match the spirit of their loyal fans to claim a famous victory in their first knockout cup final for 13 years. The Cherry & Whites overcame the disruption of a late team change on the morning of the match, with Rob Fidler replacing Mark Cornwell, to see off Northampton with a devastating second-half performance. The lead changed hands six times in the first half, but in the second Gloucester scored twenty points without reply to lift the cup.

Cries of "Glawster" were ringing round the stadium long before the kick off, but it was the Saints who posted the first score, Grayson kicking a penalty after Gloucester strayed offside at a ruck. Gloucester's response, however, was to score the first try, as James Simpson-Daniel capitalised on a loose pass by Matt Dawson inside his own 22, scooped the ball up cleanly and crossed the try line unchallenged. Mercier converted. It set the tone for the rest of the half, as scores came thick and fast at both ends. Mercier dropped a goal after Fanolua switched the direction of a Gloucester attack, but Grayson responded with two penalties as the two fly halves gave an excellent display of kicking. The second also cost Gloucester Rob Fidler for ten minutes, who was sent to the sin bin for killing the ball, and Saints took advantage with a sweeping attack. Dawson fed Grayson, who swerved past two tackles before finding full-back Beal on a well-angled run. He touched down and Grayson added a simple conversion.

Still a man short, Gloucester attacked undeterred. A delightful break by James Forrester saw him scythe through the Saints defence on the half hour. His pass to Marcel Garvey still left him to beat Beal and England wing Ben Cohen to reach the try line, but he danced round both to score. Mercier's conversion temporarily restored Gloucester lead, but by half-time they were two points adrift, Grayson kicking two further penalties to Mercier's one.

The second half saw Gloucester gradually squeeze Northampton out of the game after a crucial early try. A half break by Fanolua was stopped by the Saints defence, but two phases later, Gomarsall, Mercier and Paul combined to put Forrester in for a try in the right-hand corner. Mercier kicked the conversion to put Gloucester into a lead they were never to lose. Both sides made changes but it was Gloucester who continued to pose the greater threat, one scintillating break by Henry Paul being illegally stopped by Grayson at the expense of a yellow card. Mercier kicked the resulting penalty, and added another with nine minutes left to leave Gloucester eleven points ahead. By this stage Saints were throwing everything they had into attack, but Gloucester's rearguard effort was inspired, particularly as Thinus Delport was sent to the sin bin for obstruction. A glorious final flourish in injury time made the result safe. Dawson, who had an unhappy afternoon, saw his pass intercepted by Mercier well inside the Gloucester half. He charged clear, before sending Simpson-Daniel in for the clinching try. Mercier added the conversion, and the celebrations began.

The pattern of a season can sometimes be traced back to the one before. Teams that finish well can maintain the momentum if they pick up where they left off, especially if there has been minimal upheaval on the playing side. The reverse is also true, as a poor end to a campaign leaves a club going into the closed season on a negative note. I remember talking to Nigel Melville during the summer of 2002, and him saying how the timing of his first three months at Gloucester was crucial. He wasn't thrown into pre-season with a new set of players, or left battling against relegation with a losing side. He could assess the set-up, and in hindsight it enabled him to make some huge strides in a short space of time.

His summer shopping in terms of players was minimal. Flanker Peter Buxton was added to bring competition and versatility to the back row and Simon Amor was one for the future at half back, where he could play at either nine or ten. The one major acquisition was at full back, as Thinus Delport, a regular in the Natal side, swapped South Africa for England, and (as he thought then) said goodbye to any hopes of playing any more international rugby.

With South Africa if you go and play overseas you're not eligible to play for the Springboks. I spent a lot of sleepless nights figuring it out but I thought it was a better step for me in my rugby career. I had had four or five seasons playing in the Super 12's, and I'd seen some of the Heineken Cup on television. I was looking forward to playing in it and hoped I had made the right decision.

Subsequently of course, Springbok coach Rudi Straeuli welcomed Delport back into the fold ahead of the World Cup, based on his form for Gloucester through the season. Initially played on the wing, he looked not only more comfortable but also more dangerous at full back, showing the quality Nigel Melville knew he had.

You can develop your own and bring people through, but you need class above that. We lacked variety in our back three and Thinus added that. He had a different dimension that meant with good forwards, half backs and midfield backs we could then attack from all areas.

Good players don't always blend into a successful side, however, unless they are steered correctly, and Melville knew the back-up he wanted, although as has been detailed earlier, quality doesn't come cheaply. He retained the services of defensive coach Dave Ellis, and brought in Dean Ryan from fellow play-off finalists Bristol to work alongside him, as the pair had done at Wasps. It was a partnership that seemed to stimulate both, with Ryan concentrating on the coaching and improving the players at his disposal, and

Melville looking at his complimentary skills and the bigger picture. Their working relationship had also included time with the England Under-21s, and they felt Gloucester had the ambition to get to the top, which is where both wanted to be. Pre-season went well, with Ryan keen to make the power in the Gloucester team a bit smarter in match situations, and Melville felt Gloucester had the ingredients for a successful season.

Summer signing 2002, South African Thinus Delport. (www.gpaimages.com)

We had prepared well, and we had a core of individuals that had been at the club for a while. We had added some individuals that had fitted into that core, and that spirit is a big help. Vicks had grown in stature as a captain, he had the confidence and respect of his team-mates, and that carried a lot of weight. I had worked with good squads before but I was more excited about last season than any other.

In the overall shape of the season, the Powergen Cup is but a small part, but the way Gloucester's campaign evolved, it ended up being a huge influence. The bare fact is that a Premiership side has to win only four games to lift the Trophy, but the likelihood is that they will all be against clubs from the top division, due to the structure of the competition. Clubs are seeded according to their status, and by the time the Premiership clubs come in, only four teams from the National Leagues are left in the sixth-round draw. As it transpired, last season's two finalists, Gloucester and Northampton, both drew one of the four remaining minnows in the last sixteen.

Sixth-round Saturday was the one before Christmas, after both clubs had faced back-to-back matches in the Heineken Cup. Gloucester were battered and bruised mentally and physically after their trip to Perpignan, but the home game against Exeter, skippered by former Gloucester favourite Dave Sims, was a chance to rotate the squad and give a few people a rest. In came Catling, Collins, O'Leary, and at half back, Clive Stuart-Smith and Simon Amor. It was the England sevens specialists' Gloucester debut, and he played the full 80 minutes in a 35-6 win.

The ball was greasy in the rain. We were looking to get some passes going to give us some width, but there were quite a few errors and that prevented the flow. We weren't really direct enough and personally there wasn't enough consistency for my liking, but anyone who plays the game will tell you it's not easy if the back line hasn't played together before. That took us a while to get used to, but it was nice to be out there and to win.

The Saints' passage into the quarter-finals was far less comfortable. National Division One side Orrell gave them a real scare to the point where extra time was needed in a high-scoring match, Saints finally going through 55-44 to face Bath away in the last eight. Gloucester's draw was once again a favourable one, at home to Saracens, but just as in the sixth round the matches followed the Heineken Cup, with the group stages being completed the previous weekend. The Saints completed their Pool 6 programme against Ulster at Ravenhill. They lost 16-13, but the margin of defeat was narrow enough to ensure progress into the knockout stages, while in Pool 2 Gloucester … well …I'm sure you know. Dean Ryan felt it was now down to the players to go out against Sarries and respond.

The only way we can really speak for ourselves is by what we do for 80 minutes on a Saturday. The nature of competition is that there is a chance you may lose. It's always disappointing to lose and to nobody more than us as a group of people. You must analyse or you never learn, but we've two tournaments left and we'll now go after the Powergen Cup with all the energy we have.

One of Nigel Melville's favourite phrases is that you must 'front up' to whatever you face. This was a day where Gloucester needed a win – preferably a convincing one. Henry Paul, who would have been left out, was switched to inside centre after Robert Todd dropped out on the morning of the match, and Thinus Delport was moved to full back. He was to stay there for the rest of the season, and his two tries, along with two for James Forrester, proved the difference between good domestic and top European opposition. Gloucester won 51-20, and Delport was delighted to get things rolling in the right direction again.

It was a good confidence booster. Saracens did well at the start of the second half but it was comfortable in the end. Home advantage is worth a lot. All the Gloucester fans expect us to win at Kingsholm, and all the Munster fans expected them to win at Thomond Park. We had to show the fans that it hurt to be out of the Heineken Cup and that we were going to make it up to them by going a long way in the Powergen Cup.

Gloucester's recovery from what happened in Munster was further cemented by an away win over Saracens in the Premiership, and a hard fought 22-16 victory over Bath, who Northampton had beaten by the narrowest of margins in the Cup. It took a last-minute try by Peter Jorgensen to sneak them into the semi-finals by a single point, where they were paired with London Irish.

Financially, cup progress for Gloucester was now vital. They were back at the semi-final stage that had been their downfall so often before – just one win in the last seven attempts – but now, rather than one side having home advantage, as it had been on all those previous occasions, the venue was neutral. When Gloucester drew Leicester, Franklins Gardens was chosen, where Gloucester had won a gripping league match against the Saints in December. In that mental association of ideas, it was a ground where the Cherry & Whites had happy recent memories, and lock Mark Cornwell didn't want to miss the match even though he had a cracked bone in his thumb.

Every time we played Bath at home I seemed to break something. Last year it was an arm, this year it was my thumb. I was conscious of the cast over it, it was limiting, and I hadn't done as much work as I would have liked in the build-up. I remember talking to some of the Leicester players, and their aim was to win every game through until the end of the season. Martin Johnson is their leader and a good player too but one man doesn't make a team, and they hadn't had much joy in the Powergen Cup recently, so it was up to us to topple them over.

Forrester on fire: James gets his second try against Saracens. (www.gpaimages.com)

Gloucester did, but only just. They went for mobility in the back row with Forrester at no. 8, and the pairing of Paul and Simpson-Daniel at centre was perhaps a hint of what we may see in the future. With Phil Vickery still sidelined by injury, Andy Deacon was Gloucester's only specialist tight-head prop in the squad, and that was to cause a major talking point at the end of the match.

Leicester had a narrow 6-3 advantage at half-time, but it was Gloucester who possessed the cutting edge in the second half, with Marcel Garvey and Thinus Delport scything through the Leicester cover within four minutes of each other. Mercier kicked one conversion, and then later added a penalty that gave Gloucester that little extra cushion after Josh Kronfeld had driven over from a line-out. The real drama, however, was right at the end. Injuries to Roncero and Deacon meant two scrums under the Gloucester posts had to be uncontested. Gloucester survived and celebrated at the final whistle, but that wasn't the end of the matter after an eagle-eyed official looked at the rule book.

Rule 12.3 says 'If on the second occasion a front-row player requires to be replaced, and his team cannot provide a replacement or another player capable of playing in the front row, the referee will order uncontested scrums and the team will be deemed to have lost the match.'

It appeared a nonsense that Gloucester should be denied on a technicality when referee Steve Lander had applied common sense in ordering the uncontested scrums in the first place. A competitions sub committee chaired by Jonathan Dance decided there was insufficient justification to alter the result, but Leicester still took the option of considering an appeal. Finally, on the Wednesday after the match was played, the Tigers decided not to do so. Gloucester were into their first domestic cup final for 13 years, and no-one was more delighted than scrum-half Andy Gomarsall.

We owed it to ourselves and the management. Nobody remembers semi-final losers, we had to turn the tables from the Munster scenario, which was still there, and we did it. It was actually valuable having that experience because we didn't want to go back into the changing room having lost. We played with a good tempo and there was no panic at half-time. The forwards did their job as usual but the backs performed really well – Marcel's try was one of the tries of the season.

The Saints convincing 38-9 win over London Irish took them back to Twickenham a year after losing in the final to the same opponents – indeed Northampton had been in three finals since Gloucester's defeat by Bath in 1990, and lost them all. Gloucester had no such baggage, but the match looked a close one to call. Gloucester had won both Premiership matches between the teams, but the victories were narrow, and there was still no Phil Vickery because of injury.

Tickets sold rapidly at both clubs. Gloucester accounted for more than 22,000 themselves, although estimates on the day put the Cherry & Whites support in excess of 30,000 by the time fans who had made independent arrangements were accounted for. A fleet of coaches left Kingsholm on the morning of the match, and also trying to get through the traffic was Rob Fidler.

I had a call from Pete Glanville at about 8.15 to say that Mark Cornwell had been up in the night feeling sick. I wasn't in the 22 so I was going to watch the final with my family. I had expected a lazy morning, packing the car and then driving up. Glanners said he'd ring again at 9.00, and at that stage he said I was definitely needed. He arranged a lift with Dr Kirwin, and an hour later having grabbed my suit and kit, we were on our way. I knew I was playing by about 1 o'clock. It wasn't a problem other than I'd had three or four lagers the night before! I felt sorry for Mark but it was an opportunity I had to grab with both hands.

It was a disruption to Nigel Melville's plans but only a minor one. Cornwell, Fidler and Adam Eustace had been consistent performers throughout the season – although normally the line-out calling was Cornwell's responsibility – and Fidler was the most experienced player in the squad in terms of League appearances. The back row that had served Gloucester so well in the semi-final was retained, Trevor Woodman's return to fitness at prop was appropriately timed, and the pace of James Simpson-Daniel was switched to the wing to allow Terry Fanolua to partner Henry Paul at centre. It looked a strong side but Nigel Melville accepted that Northampton would fancy their chances too.

We were very similar sides. In the front five we maybe shaded them and in the back row they maybe shaded us a bit. It looked pretty even at half back, although they had more experience, in the midfield, we possibly had the edge, and the back three looked even again. We had the advantage of having been to Twickenham recently and won, and a positive frame of mind is vital. No-one remembers who comes second – show me someone who comes second and I'll show you a loser.

It was again down to Jake Boer to lead the team in the continuing absence of Vickery. The South African had become a popular figure for his hard graft and consistency of performance, and only Fanolua had started more matches for Gloucester during the

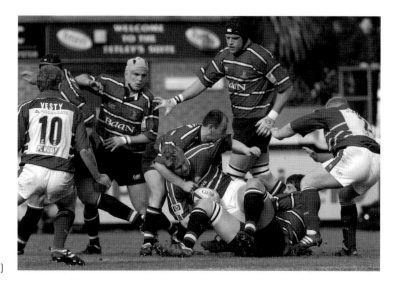

Outnumbered:
Leicester's Ollie
Smith is tackled by
Rob Fidler and
Ludovic Mercier.
(www.gpaimages.com)

season. Boer was a hot favourite to become player of the year, an accolade he not only achieved at Kingsholm but also across the Premiership, although as a captain he's an undemonstrative individual.

I just try to give 100 per cent and hope that sets the guys around me on fire. I'm not a big talker. As a captain, I have to try and make the right decisions but having support makes the skipper's job easier. The game does go quickly so you just have to soak up what you can of it on the day, but if you want to make it to the top the most important thing is to perform.

I can remember arriving early at Twickenham on Saturday 5 April, and being grateful that the radio commentary positions were in the West Stand. It was a gorgeous day, and fans with tickets in the East Stand would have no escape from the sun. The car parks were rapidly filling up with supporters five hours before kick off, and the tradition of the picnic lunch out the car boot was soon in full swing. Inside the ground, particularly as the Intermediate Cup and Powergen Shield finals were in progress, the swathe of colour grew. The cherry and white swept round to our left in the North Stand, with the green, gold and black of the Saints largely to our right, although there was no rigorous segregation. Replica shirts were very much in evidence, and the many different designs showed the loyalty of the Gloucester fans. It's not inconceivable that some of the shirts had been worn to the club's last final thirteen years before. The unusual element of the day was that the match was the last of four finals to be played, leaving the players no time for a gentle amble on the pitch in order to acclimatise themselves with the atmosphere. Instead it was a brisk jog behind the in goal area at the North Stand end, and then a few drills once the Shield final was over. Chris Catling was one of the ones not playing who observed it all from the touchline.

I was the twenty-third member of the squad for the final – in effect, the travelling reserve. I had that job a few times during the season. You're there just in case someone drops out at the last minute, which of course Pasty did but that was no good for me! I was still in my suit because I

GLOUCESTER

This team was accurate on 3 April 2003

POWERGEN

NORTHAMPTON SAINTS

This team was accurate on 3 April 2003

Gloucester		Position		Northampton Saints
15	THINUS DELPORT	FULL BACK	NICK BEAL	15
14	MARCEL GARVEY	RIGHT WING	BRUCE REIHANA	14
13	TERRY FANOLUA	CENTRE	PETER JORGENSEN	13
12	HENRY PAUL	CENTRE	(CO-CAPTAIN) JOHN LESLIE	12
11	JAMES SIMPSON–DANIEL	LEFT WING	BEN COHEN	11
10	LUDOVIC MERCIER	FLY HALF	PAUL GRAYSON	10
9	ANDY GOMARSALL	SCRUM HALF	MATT DAWSON	9
1	TREVOR WOODMAN	PROP	TOM SMITH	1
2	OLIVIER AZAM	HOOKER	STEVE THOMPSON	2
3	ANDY DEACON	PROP	ROBBIE MORRIS	3
4	ADAM EUSTACE	LOCK	MATT LORD	4
5	MARK CORNWELL	LOCK	STEVE WILLIAMS	5
6	JAKE BOER (CAPTAIN)	FLANKER	MARK CONNORS	6
7	ANDY HAZELL	FLANKER	(CO-CAPTAIN) BUDGE POUNTNEY	7
8	JAMES FORRESTER	NO.8	ANDREW BLOWERS	8

GLOUCESTER RFC

REPLACEMENTS

16	CLIVE STUART-SMITH
17	SIMON AMOR
18	ROBERT TODD
19	CHRIS FORTEY
20	RODRIGO RONCERO
21	JUNIOR PARAMORE
22	ED PEARCE

REPLACEMENTS

DAN RICHMOND	16
MATTIE STEWART	17
GRANT SEELY	18
DARREN FOX	19
JOHNNY HOWARD	20
JAMES BROOKS	21
CHRIS HYNDMAN	22

Score		
Tries	Conv.	Penalties
Drop Goals		

Referee: **Tony Spreadbury** can be heard today on **Ref!Link**

Touch Judges: **Ashley Reay** & **Stuart Terheerge**

No 4: **Steve Leyshon**

Score		
Tries	Conv.	Penalties
Drop Goals		

wasn't going to be pulled in to cover a second row. You almost act happy externally for the benefit of the team in that situation but inside I was gutted not to be playing.

The expectation when the teams came out was as huge as the roar that greeted them. Here were two strong traditional clubs with good core support creating an atmosphere that had a different crackle to that of an international. Nigel Melville's programme notes referred to is as 'a celebration of the best in English club rugby'. He wasn't wrong. The first half came and went in a flash, which is always a good indication of the quality of the match. Both sides made mistakes but enjoyed spells in the ascendancy, and Gloucester had scored two tries to the Saints one. It seemed inconceivable that the pace of the action and the scoring could continue for another forty minutes, but James Forrester's try at the start of the second half suggested otherwise. Thereafter however, it was Gloucester who established the better pattern. Gradually they exerted a level of control and Mercier's goals gave them a cushion. The clock was almost up when Simpson-Daniel sped away for the clinching score, whereupon I, and probably every Gloucester supporter in the ground, felt the stands physically shake. You could feel the floor moving beneath your feet as the realisation of what had happened hit home. The pain of the Munster defeat and the rumours over the clubs financial affairs were swept aside. Gloucester had won the Powergen Cup.

What followed, of course, substantially enhanced Jake Boer's status as a man to the Kingsholm regulars. He may have been captain for the day, but it was Andy Deacon who collected the cup, the veteran prop raising it skywards to a crescendo of fireworks and thunderous cheering. The Saints had played their part, but three players who had come through the Gloucester Academy had scored the tries that won the cup, James Simpson-Daniel getting the first as well as the last.

If you ask any of the boys it wasn't about who scored, it was about winning. We didn't want a slow, quiet game, but if that had happened I would have been happy so long as we won. Northampton attacked tactically and it was close at half-time but there was no panic and we got

OPPOSITE PAGE:

Matchday programme: the two teams from the final. Mark Cornwell was replaced by Rob Fidler on the day.

LEFT:

Wing Marcel Garvey tries to escape the clutches of Saints' Matt Dawson.
(www.gpaimages.com)

BELOW:

French fly-half Ludovic Mercier lands a second-half penalty.
(www.gpaimages.com)

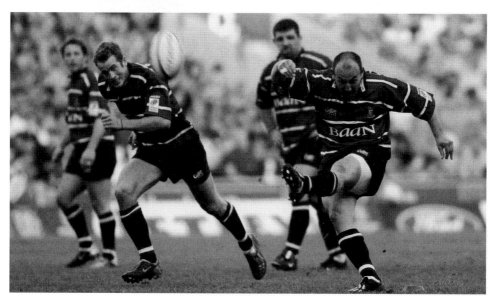

ourselves together. The crowd were magnificent. Halfway through the second half I could hear them chanting and when you are as tired as you can be, it really lifts you.

The victory meant hooker Olivier Azam returned home to France at the end of the season with a cup winner's medal. He felt fitness played a part in the result.

We put a lot of desire into the game and maybe did some damage in the first half because they had cramp later on. The first half was like a Barbarians game. In the second half we played more territory and made more effort in defence. When you defend well you are under less pressure and it is easier to keep the discipline. It was a great day, especially for Deacs. He is a top prop, even better than some I have seen in the Six Nations.

The result meant Nigel Melville had steered the club to securing a major trophy in his first full season.

We have some very special players, and when we played they couldn't stop us. It was frustrating that everything they got in the first half, we gave them. We were playing from stupid, deep positions and we needed to get up the field. The players took that on board at half-time and you saw the result. It was a really special day.

The players lived on the euphoria of the result right through until the open-top bus tour through the centre of Gloucester nine days later. That period included a home game against Newcastle, where a 20-point deficit was finally hauled in by a Thinus Delport try in injury time, and Mercier's conversion maintained the 100 per cent home record. The tour took place at lunchtime, but still the fans turned out in their thousands. Top spot in the league was secured by a high-scoring draw at Sale and a home win over Harlequins, where fittingly the fourth Gloucester try that secured the bonus point was scored by Ludovic Mercier, the club's top point scorer and another set to depart the scene. The defeat in the last away game at Leeds was the first for nine games, but the Kingsholm season was finished with a flourish by beating Leicester. Gloucester's final points tally from their twenty-two Premiership matches was eighty-two – fifteen more than runners-up Wasps – although the rules said they got nothing for it.

The Premiership Trophy would be played for on Saturday 31 May between the top team in the league, and the winners of the play off between the second and third placed clubs. Wasps were also in the final of the Parker Pen Shield, and having two competitive games ahead of the Zurich final was plainly an advantage when it came to what should have been a showpiece finale. Wasps had beaten Sale to reach Twickenham, and beaten Bath to win the Parker Pen Shield. They were sharp and confident. Gloucester's season had ended three weeks earlier, and the break had done them no good at all. When Stuart Abbott burst through the Gloucester cover to create a try for Josh Lewsey within two minutes, the signs were ominous. A solitary Mercier penalty was all Gloucester could muster, and the match was over as a contest long before the end. Wasps won 39-3. It was almost like the Bath experience thirteen years before … which is, of course, where we started.

The squad realise the dream of winning the Powergen Cup. (www.gpaimages.com)

City centre joy: the players parade the cup through Gloucester on an open-top bus. (www.gpaimages.com)

ONWARDS AND UPWARDS

In 2004, Gloucester Rugby Club is 131 years old. They will have played on the same ground for 113 years, and although the shirt design may have changed in modern times, Gloucester's colours have been red and white since the club borrowed a set of kit from Painswick Rugby Club in the 1800s. The village side truly were the original 'cherry and whites', but while they compete this season in the Gloucestershire Premier Division, their near neighbours are now, in rugby terms, a world away. The numbers on the shirts may be the same, but that's about all.

Painswick have a modern club house at Broad Ham, which they share with the village cricket team, and their base and immediate future look reasonably settled. Predicting what might happen at Gloucester is rather more difficult, not just because of their affairs, but because everything has to be put into context against what is happening at the other leading clubs.

Nigel Melville is the club's chief plate spinner on the playing side. Despite the financial belts being tightened, he is still expected to deliver a winning formula on the field in a way that will keep the crowds rolling in. Melville has built up his stock after winning the Zurich play offs in 2002 and the Powergen Cup last season, but this time round, like most of the other directors of rugby in the Premiership, he has had to cope without a handful of star names through the autumn because of the World Cup, and he's honest enough to know the tournament will have a big impact on the league come the finale in the spring.

You're always looking at this job on three levels. I would like to think we'd be in the top half of the table at the end of the World Cup, and our players would come back with no serious injuries. We would then be in a good position for the second half of the season, which is also important because you are then recruiting for 2004/05. I also hope a lot of the younger players who will have had a bigger role in the first team will have become prominent members of the squad. That will give us more depth, and then you look at where you need players from outside to perhaps cover those who are leaving the cycle at the top, especially if they are in positions where we are short. It's an ongoing process and it never stops.

It's hard to believe that Marcel Garvey had made only one replacement appearance in the Premiership before the start of last season, and that Melville warned him he might not last more than another year with Gloucester unless he sharpened up his game. The difference in twelve months has been huge, with Garvey being a regular selection at club level, as well as playing for England A and being picked for his country in the Under-21 World Cup. His progress alone gives Melville confidence in what he is doing, especially as it is a mirror image of the system he used so successfully at Wasps.

Determined duo: director of rugby Nigel Melville and club captain Jake Boer in the new kit.
(www.gpaimages.com)

Integrating the less experienced players into the Gloucester team will be down to Melville and his coach Dean Ryan on the training ground, but in match situations that responsibility is handed to the captain and his senior players. Jake Boer, the 28-year-old South African flanker, relished the responsibility last season when Phil Vickery was injured, and with the giant prop out of the equation for the early part of the season, continuity made him the natural choice to lead the team. Boer had had little experience of captaining a side since playing for the Villager club in Cape Town at Under-21 level, but you wouldn't have known, and he wants the club to build on the foundations laid down over last season.

All the other teams will be out to beat us now, but that's natural after you have finished top of the Premiership table. Our approach is the same, because we want to win every game too and if we do that we'll either be at the top or very close to it. As we saw last season, some teams start well, and some finish well. The key is to be consistent. A few guys left in the summer, including some key players, but we made some signings to cover the spots as best we could. My thing has always been to lead by example, and that if there is a tough spot in a game I'm the one to lead the guys out of it. As players all we want is to win, and I'm sure the supporters feel the same. The way we paid them back was by doing what we did last season, but the biggest challenge for us is to stay at that level and it's going to take a real team effort.

In terms of any pecking order when it comes to silverware, it could be argued that winning the Powergen Cup is the logical stepping stone to greater glory. Just four wins

The men in charge: chairman Tom Walkinshaw (right) and managing director Ken Nottage. (Bruce Seabrook/www.gpaimages.com)

are necessary to secure it, significantly fewer than any other competition. The usual yardstick for players, management and supporters alike is the league, but increasingly the glamour and level of competition in Europe has turned the Heineken Cup into the ultimate prize. This season's group stages are played after the World Cup, and with bonus points now on offer (bringing the pool stages in line with the Premiership) former skipper Phil Vickery is expecting the excitement to match Gloucester's previous seasons in the competition.

The Heineken Cup is the big thing to me because it's the highest level you can play at with your club. I've said before there are no weak sides and you want to be in it every year because that's the only way you learn how to play against these teams and compete with them. Days like the quarter-final against Cardiff in 2001 are special. Kingsholm was teeming and it was brilliant to be involved and to beat another traditional club with good players in a good team. The bonus points will make a difference. It was so close for us last year, and you want to get through to the quarter-finals. Qualifying through the pool stages will give a buzz to everyone.

What happened in Limerick in January 2003 has been dealt with elsewhere, but it's relevant to look at the order for this season's pool stages. Gloucester start and end with games against Treviso, and director of rugby Nigel Melville is far more comfortable with playing the Italians last than either Munster or Bourgoin.

It's still a tough group — in fact I'm amazed how tough it is — but at least the order of matches is better than last time. My problem is the gap between the first two games and the last four. I would like to run the group stages straight through. You are picking up teams at different points with different form and different selections, so it's important not to lose the focus. Munster have added a few like Christian Cullen, and season on season you can never tell what's going to happen. There won't be a try fest like we had against Viadana last season, but we might need to win the last game by a certain number of points, and Treviso at home is certainly better than Munster away, that's for sure.

Jake Boer also feels a good win in the first pool match is vital.

You have to start well or you're on the back foot immediately, especially with our group. The games against Munster and Bourgoin will be huge because of the history there. Philippe had a good time here and is coming back, and although it's not a grudge match it's one he would love to win, and the Munster game was one of the key ones we picked out from last season. Treviso might just put a spanner in the works too and we mustn't slip up like we did last year.

The big question, is of course, are Gloucester ready? The job of Nigel Melville and Dean Ryan is to keep the squad a step ahead of the opposition, even if the core of the squad remains the same. There were just four major summer signings — lock Alex Brown, outside-half Duncan McRae, and two experienced front-row forwards in Paul Johnstone and Steve Brotherstone — but Melville believes he and Ryan have still got plenty to work with.

We haven't touched what is possible. Just about everything is different compared to when Philippe was here. The training, conditioning, tactics, the way we analyse games, we run the whole team differently even though the raw material we are working with is very similar. The important element to me is balance. You must have experience in certain areas but youth brings enthusiasm. Older players carry baggage and young players have less fear. I check out anybody who we sign, because sometimes what they offer in training and in terms of team spirit can be greater than their worth as a player alone. Not all our players are the best but they can be more effective as people than others who are better than them. We can't afford to carry a big squad now and we've had to double up in certain areas to make things fit, but in the long run I think it will benefit the club, and we've already identified some 17-year-olds who we want in the squad for next year.

It would have been hard on the verge of last season to predict the impact Marcel Garvey would have. The balance of first-team appearances this season will have a very different slant by the end, and while Simon Amor, Josh Frape and Jon Goodridge have already been exposed to the Premiership, there are a clutch of younger players who will learn a lot this season, among them Brad Davies. He went to the Under-21 World Cup last summer with England, and Phil Vickery has known him since he was fourteen.

I first met Brad when Phil Greening and I used to do some coaching at Spartans. Even then he looked to have all the skills you need. Mark Rimmer was there too and he's in the Academy now. I've also seen what Ryan Lamb is capable of doing, but now they all have to make the step into the big world, and it can be hard. Sometimes young players can do OK to start with but then people note your name and it becomes tougher. I think they will be good enough, but it's up them to prove their worth.

Jake Boer believes the management of the young players is crucial in their development.

A coach has to read when a player is coming through and pick him when he's ready. Some young players do that quite quickly when they are young and in only a few games they become much better, but for others it's the worst thing that has ever happened to them. We are working towards the same aim from top to bottom, but ultimately it is the responsibility of the coach to judge if a player will get a first-team chance and then take it.

As the game has evolved professionally, the Gloucester squad has gone from a locally based set of forwards with a cosmopolitan back division to (inevitably) one with a greater cultural spread, given the fact it was being run by an internationally renowned star in Philippe Saint-André. His departure has seen home-based talent come to the fore again but that doesn't mean Nigel Meville has turned his back on signing overseas players. The Argentine Juan-Martin Hernandez has been high on his wanted list for some time, but Melville could yet lose his man to Stade Français, who want to team up Hernandez with his countryman Augustin Pichot at half back. Ultimately, all Melville wants is success for Gloucester, whether it is achieved through signing English players or not.

I would rather have English players if we can have them all the time, but England put more demands on the players than any nation other than Australia and New Zealand, where the players are 'owned' by the Union. I want a team that plays how we want them to for Gloucester, but if we can't have those players for 50 per cent of the matches we're not going to achieve it. With skills days and training days the access for the club is less and less, and it gets to the stage where there is little value in having them at all.

The finale to this season, given the disruption the World Cup will have caused, promises to be one of the most exciting in the history of the Premiership, and if it can match the mathematical puzzle that existed at the bottom of the table last May, then the game as a whole can only gain as a result. Phil Vickery has spent virtually the whole of 2003 out of a Gloucester shirt, first because of injury, and latterly because of international calls, but no-one wants to keep the winning habit more than the man to win more England caps while playing for Gloucester than any other player.

Anyone who says they know who is going to win this or that is clutching at straws. A lot of teams will come through that people don't expect, and I think there is more pressure on us now because we HAVE achieved something. Last season we had a good start with five wins and a draw from the first six games and that makes such a difference. You're not always going to win, but there's no reason why we can't compete at the top. I want us to give ourselves a chance going into the last three or four games, although in the long term it will be difficult to achieve the dominance of a Bath and a Leicester. Bath were almost professional before their time and Leicester are a well-run club who had a nucleus of players who all grew up together. They will still be a threat, but now there is nobody who is head and shoulders above everybody else. It's about getting a run going and being consistent.

It would be good if when we get to the end of the season we're not looking back as much at the off-the-field affairs at Kingsholm as those on it. Both Melville and Vickery expressed their desire to stay out of the politics as much as possible, although Melville admitted it was difficult at times not to get involved. At this stage I would have liked some input from Tom Walkinshaw in terms of some overall forward-thinking strategy, but despite trying for six weeks to secure the chairman he was unavailable for comment. Purely from a playing point of view, however, the director of rugby, the current captain and the former captain are all optimistic that the success the club enjoyed in 2002/03 isn't a one off.

Nigel Melville: *For me it's the little things that make the team tick, for example players staying behind to work on their skills, putting in commitment in training, looking after themselves, generally being professional. I like the players to have an input either directly or through Jake [Boer] which helps them to buy into the team picture, and that is hugely important. Last season was one where we learned to live with pressure. This season nobody will expect more than me.*

Jake Boer: *We've tried to create a whole new game by bringing new elements in. Some teams didn't work us out last year, but a few noticed what we were doing and so we've got to try and be one step ahead again. Sometimes you make changes and they don't work, or you work on certain areas for specific opposition. There will be a few younger guys in the team this season but there are still enough who can help me with the decision making, and I would like to think we'll be in the top three when we finish the group stages of the Heineken Cup.*

Phil Vickery: *I really hope this club is at the start of a long and successful ladder. We still have so much to achieve, and anyone who has feelings and was involved in the final game of last season will want to go out and put that right. Last year we used everybody in the squad and we had a good blend, a good work ethic and some great off-field staff. I was disappointed when Wayne Diesel and some of the players left in the summer, and it's sad that Rudi Meir won't be around either. I just hope these people that leave go wherever they go in the world and tell everybody what a great place Gloucester is for rugby, because I don't think you'll find anywhere better.*

Never mind that Phil Vickery is 6ft 3in and 19 stones. For supporters of rugby in its most traditional form, Gloucester is a city where that's an argument which is hard to dispute.

STATISTICS

Domestic Cup records (as at 1 September 2003)

Season	Stage reached	Result
1971/72	Winners	Gloucester 17 Moseley 6
1972/73	2nd Round	Bristol 16 Gloucester 11
1973/74	2nd Round	Gloucester 9 London Scottish 12
1974/75	2nd Round	Moseley 10 Gloucester 7
1975/76	2nd Round	Sale 16 Gloucester 15
1976/77	Quarter-final	Gosforth 3 Gloucester 0
1977/78	Winners	Gloucester 6 Leicester 3
1978/79	1st Round	Gloucester 3 Richmond 3 (note 1)
1979/80	Quarter-final	Gloucester 3 Rosslyn Park 6
1980/81	Quarter-final	London Scottish 9 Gloucester 9 (note 2)
1981/82	Joint winners	Gloucester 12 Moseley 12 (note 3)
1982/83	1st Round	Gloucester 3 London Welsh 14
1983/84	Did not qualify	
1984/85	Semi-final	Gloucester 11 Bath 12
1985/86	Quarter-final	London Scottish 12 Gloucester 8
1986/87	Quarter-final	Orrell 16 Gloucester 10
1987/88	4th Round	Gloucester 13 Wasps 24
1988/89	Semi-final	Gloucester 3 Bath 6
1989/90	Final	Bath 48 Gloucester 6
1990/91	4th Round	Gloucester 13 Harlequins 15
1991/92	Semi-final	Gloucester 18 Bath 27
1992/93	3rd Round	Newcastle Gosforth 13 Gloucester 10
1993/94	Quarter-final	Gloucester 3 Orrell 10
1994/95	4th Round	Wakefield 19 Gloucester 9
1995/96	Semi-final	Bath 19 Gloucester 10
1996/97	Semi-final	Gloucester 13 Leicester 26
1997/98	5th Round	Northampton 30 Gloucester 11
1998/99	Semi-final	Wasps 35 Gloucester 21
1999/00	Quarter-final	London Irish 31 Gloucester 18
2000/01	5th Round	Gloucester 13 Leicester 25
2001/02	Quarter-final	London Irish 25 Gloucester 10
2002/03	Winners	Gloucester 40 Northampton 22

Note 1 – Richmond go through as away team / Note 2 – London Scottish go through on tries scored
Note 3 – Trophy shared

European records (as at 1 September 2003)

Season	Competition	Stage reached	Result
1996/97	European Conf.	Group	n/a
1997/98	European Conf.	Quarter-final	Stade Français 53 Gloucester 22
1998/99		English clubs did not enter	
1999/00	European Shield	Group	n/a
2000/01	Heineken Cup	Semi-final	Gloucester 15 Leicester 19
2001/02	European Shield	Semi-final	Gloucester 27 Sale 28
2002/03	Heineken Cup	Group	n/a

Seasonal League Records (as at 1 September 2003)

Season	Final Position	Played	Won	Drawn	Lost	Pts For	Pts Against
1987/88	5th	10	6	1	3	206	121
1988/89	2nd	11	7	1	3	215	112
1989/90	2nd	11	8	1	2	214	139
1990/91	6th	12	6	0	6	207	163
1991/92	4th	12	7	1	4	193	168
1992/93	5th	12	6	0	6	173	151
1993/94	8th	18	6	2	10	247	356
1994/95	7th	18	6	1	11	269	336
1995/96	8th	18	6	0	12	275	370
1996/97	7th	22	11	1	10	476	589
1997/98	7th	22	11	1	10	512	528
1998/99	10th	26	9	1	16	554	643
1999/00	3rd	22	15	0	7	628	490
2000/01	7th	22	10	0	12	473	526
2001/02	3rd	22	14	0	8	692	485
2002/03	1st	22	17	2	3	617	396
Overall Home Record		141	100	4	37	3452	2257
Overall Away Record		139	45	8	86	2499	3316

Current Squad Premiership records
(correct at 1 September 2003)

Name	Debut	Appearances	Rep. Apps.	Points
Andy Deacon	1991/92	124	20	40
Terry Fanolua	1997/98	108	4	130
Chris Fortey	1996/97	56	47	15
Mark Cornwell	1994/95	73	29	35
Trevor Woodman	1996/97	65	23	50
Phil Vickery	1996/97	62	14	20
Junior Paramore	1999/00	61	6	90
Jake Boer	2000/01	61	3	60
Andy Gomarsall	2000/01	52	8	63
Adam Eustace	1998/99	34	23	25
Andy Hazell	1997/98	28	25	25
Robert Todd	2000/01	37	5	30
Henry Paul	2001/02	32	4	112
James Forrester	2000/02	27	7	55
James Simpson-Daniel	2000/01	20	12	55
Marcel Garvey	2001/02	16	4	35
Thinus Delport	2002/03	17	3	10
Peter Buxton	2002/03	5	11	0
Rodrigo Roncero	2002/03	10	2	5
Jon Goodridge	2000/01	2	2	0
Josh Frape	2001/02	1	2	0
Simon Amor	2002/03	1	2	9
Adam Caves	2002/03	0	1	0
Rob Elloway	2002/03	0	1	0
Chris Collins	2002/03	1	0	0
Nick Cox	2000/01	0	1	0
Luke Narraway	2002/03	1	0	0
Steve Brotherstone				
Alex Brown				
Brad Davies				
Mark Foster				
Paul Johnstone				
Duncan McRae				
Alex Page				